Wanted:

My life on the run as Billy Yates

William Martindale

With

Paul Knight & Jamie O'Keefe

New Breed Productions

2

Copyright Billy Martindale 2008 ©

Published by New Breed publishing

Printed in Dec 2008 (2nd print)

Printed by

New Breed Publishing
Po box 2676
Romford
Essex RM7 OWA
www.newbreedbooks.co.uk

A CIP catalogue record for this book is available from the
British Library
Printed and bound in Great Britain.

- **ISBN-10:** 1904432417

- **ISBN-13:** 978-1904432418

Please note: The theoretical information and physical
techniques outlined in this book are for information
purposes only. The authors and the publishers cannot accept
any responsibility for any proceedings or prosecutions
brought or instituted against any person or body as a result
of the misuse of any theoretical information or physical
techniques described in this book or any loss, injury or
damage caused thereby.

DEDICATIONS

This book is dedicated to my dad and my hero, my mother Jean, brother Glynn, and sisters Vicky, Joanne, Sarah Jane, Danielle, my good pals Jamie O'Keefe, Paul Knight (for putting up with me lol) for having the balls to put my book in print where others feared to tread, Mickey Nesbitt, Mark Brandon 'chopper' Read & his lovely wife Margaret.

My ex-partners in crime, Paul Meeking, Robert Josephs, Christopher Donnelly, Neil Charles and Ray Ogwood.

Tommy shepherd (rip), Simon Paul Taylor (rip) Ian Jones (rip), Jim Thorpe, Gordon - my website man, Roy 'pretty boy' Shaw, Billy frost, Lenny Hamilton, Mickey Bennett, Mark Emmins, Tom and Rose Shepherd , all of tom's brothers, Mr. Kent and Mr. Robinson - my old school teachers , Mr. Dring for caning me, Janet and Theo, and last but not least my lovely fiery partner Tina, my sons Reece and Lewis and my beautiful princess Lilly xxxx

Special mention to Billy and Eddie Blundell, John 'Gaffa' Rollinson, Danny Woollard, Chris Stafford, Jim from my local pub and a big thanks to Dave at international firearms.

Jamie O'Keefe for his lovable arrogance and being the most honest and likeable man I know who keeps his toughness well hidden!

Paul knight for helping me understand that tolerance and understanding gets things done opposed to violence (most of the time LOL) .

And to the drug dealers who helped me when I was a bit strapped for cash... by allowing them to be robbed by me.

And all those others who stood by me through thick and thin.

DISCLAIMER

This book was created from a combination of conversations, one-to-one interviews and specifically submitted written contributions from William Martindale. Where possible we have used word for word extracts that are clearly marked from the contributor so you can get an essence of the contributors' specific and unique character and style.

The authors have pieced this book together based on the information given by Mr. Martindale, and we would like to express that the thoughts and ideas presented are solely Mr. Martindale's and are not the opinions of the authors.

Every effort was made to verify the facts provided but in some cases it was deemed more appropriate to change certain aspects to protect those that may be affected by what has been transcribed from the documented tape recordings, letters and emails of Mr. Martindale.

All testimonials, comments and quotes were all provided through Mr. Martindale and have been presented throughout as factual citations from the sources described. They have not been changed in any way by the authors or publisher.

A majority of the photos used throughout this book are the copyright of the Martindale family and permission was granted for the use of them. All efforts were made to contact the rightful owners of the photos used that did not originate from the Martindale family and where found, permission was granted to use them in this publication.

We would like to thank those that helped with the creation of this book.

To my true friend Billy Yates,

"You cannot choose your battlefield--God will do that for you, but you can fly your flag where no flag ever flew"

Your friend always
Mark Brandon "Chopper" Read.

INTRODUCTION

My name is William Martindale; I was named by my mother Jean and dad Lewis, after my granddad William, or bill as he was known. The police have known me by many names during my life, I was always a forward and funny child, even from the age of 3 as my dad still has a cassette tape somewhere he recorded, and listening to that makes me laugh. I do not blame anyone in particular for the way I have been , I think I'm a product of my environment, and some days I feel I should put something back in society, and other days or even hours later I think 'nah fuck em'.

I know I'm not on everyone's Xmas card list and I do not blame anyone in particular for the way I have been, but I do feel that I'm a product of my environment. I can be William and I can be Billy, I have done some bad things to mostly bad people, I have suffered the mental torture of a sick and twisted stepmother, and at that time unbeknown to him she was normal, but I knew another side, I clashed with my father so much and sometimes still do, but hey he's my dad and I love him.... He played the cards he had been dealt in life and did his best with us kids and that are my reason why I was always proud of my dad. He was my hero and still is, well sometimes. But I don't let him know as often as I should.

My life so far has been a rollercoaster of hate, anger, suicides, death, guns, stabbings, kidnappings, torture, abuse, prison, deaths of pals, murders of pals, you fucking name it it's been in my life.... people have constantly let me down throughout my life in one way or another, and I usually push them away first before they get in to close to me, and there is not many people I truly like. If you wrong me I can turn on you in an instant and follow through with anything you want. I will never stop or forget if you hurt me, I will hunt you, like the mongrel wankers who have wronged me in the past, must remember I will never forget you, and you know who you are, time is on my side and when winter draws in I will be sitting in your shadows, even if I have to wait twenty fucking years from now, that's why I prefer animals to people , if a dog shits on my floor or has a bite at me, that's its instinct or emotion that causes it to have done that, not malice or cunning to rip you off or hurt you.

I like what you see is what you get, not theses two faces cunts who are cowards, or false friends, liars, give me a fucking ferret and a Jack Russell any day over a person. I could live on a mountain top with just my family and never see another person again, yet the other side of me loves to be loved, and needs to make you smile and happy, if you're sitting here reading this frowning with no understanding of what I'm babbling on about, how the fuck do you think I feel?

So please read on and enjoy.... and if you come to the end and you decide you don't like it then just sell the cunting book on eBay or give it to fucking charity.

Enjoy

Billy Yates / William Martindale

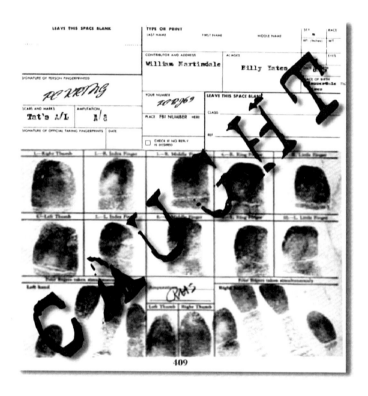

LEAVE THIS SPACE BLANK

TYPE OR PRINT
LAST NAME   FIRST NAME   MIDDLE NAME   SEX   RACE
HT (Inches)   WT

CONTRIBUTOR AND ADDRESS
William Martindale

ALIASES
Billy Yates

SIGNATURE OF PERSON FINGERPRINTED

JC KING

SCARS AND MARKS   AMPUTATION
Tat's N/L   N/S

SIGNATURE OF OFFICIAL TAKING FINGERPRINTS   DATE

YOUR NUMBER
108969

PLACE FBI NUMBER HERE

LEAVE THIS SPACE BLANK
CLASS
REF

CHECK IF NO REPLY IS DESIRED

1.—Right Thumb   2.—R. Index Finger   3.—R. Middle Finger   4.—R. Ring Finger   5.—R. Little Finger

6.—Left Thumb   7.—L. Index Finger   8.—L. Middle Finger   9.—L. Ring Finger   10.—L. Little Finger

Four Fingers taken simultaneously
Left Hand

Left Thumb   Right Thumb

Four Fingers taken simultaneously
Right Hand

409

CHAPTER 1

In a world where a criminal is revered by those who have never walked a step in that realm and your average thug can be classed as a celebrity, it is no wonder that the hype that follows those that happily put on paper for all to read that they would walk through hell to take revenge on those foolish enough to cross them gains them household notoriety for all the wrong reasons. In the last decade there have been countless books written by and about infamous people that have made a mark within the British criminal underworld whether it is with good reason, somewhat fictional or just someone riding another person's coattails. All those subject matter's reassuring their own vanity by issuing wild claims of never losing a fight even though they fought over a 1000, being the equivalent to a god in organised crime or part of a feared gang of cold bloodied killers, how could you even start to believe that you should expect honesty from a book focusing on a criminal, gangster, fighter, drug dealer, murderer and alike? In 2007, a book was published about an unlicensed fighter who had been cheated out of a chance to prove he was the rightful guv'nor of that brutal profession, the title was 'Wild Thing' and it told the story of Lew Yates, a very large and dangerous man who used his fists to tackle all that the world could throw at him. What made this book different to those that would fall within the same category as laying the foundation to the 'Big I am' genre was its honesty towards how Lew's personal life crumbled through tragedies with love, family and money troubles, highlighting his vulnerability and weaknesses whilst having to maintain that strong image to those whose opinions would never even factor in to his life. Perception is everything, reputation is paramount and a failing is something you can never let others know about, Lew's story was both refreshing and candid and showed that no matter what image you are out to project to the outside world, even the toughest person can succumb to sorrow, betrayal and a broken heart.

I had already read 'wild thing' and had spoken to Lew a few times before I had even heard from his offspring, Billy 'Yates', regarding him following in his dad's footsteps in not only him adopting the pseudo name of 'Yates' instead of holding the true family name of Martindale but also producing a book about his life that had seen him on the run from the police for a total of 16 years. Billy contacted me back in April 2008, to write his account of events that had been laid out there for anyone to read within his father's printed life story as well as his own journey through time amongst the same criminal figures that had already had their lives chronicled in print. In the months that followed after I agreed to pen his biography, our relationship hit rock bottom, the future of this book coming to existence seemed more and more less likely as I endured countless threats, slanderous accusations and school yard name calling. Mutual friends could not believe the abuse that was thrown my way by the vindictive Billy Yates who made it public that he wanted to 'bury me', this was a man who was renowned for having a violent temperament, documented friendships with some of the UK's most deadliest people and a couldn't give a fuck attitude to life. Disassociating me from such a negative person seemed the most logical thing to do before I got dragged down to his level and be forced to become the very person I have spent years readjusting from and as I proceeded to, the threats, abuse and public slurring got worse and it was through these actions that between the gaps I stopped seeing the rampaging bully that was Billy Yates and started seeing the insecure and vulnerable man that was William (Billy) Martindale. It was this man's story I finally agreed to get back on board and write this book alongside my good friend and business partner, Jamie O'Keefe. I explored what made this man tick and found that it wasn't so much the survival nature of a man having to defend and provide whilst running from incarceration but his childhood and upbringing that shaped his views, reactions and evident uncertainties that haunt him. Although the original format and direction of the intended book has changed I can only hope that as you read this, you will still see the unflinching characteristics of his alter ego, Billy Yates but also get a better understanding as to why he projects this persona when his true nature is that of a man full of insecurities, doubt and longing for trust.

I have thought long and hard on how to start this journey, what words should I use to grab the reader's attention as I introduce you to the person that this book centres on, I thought I might start with one of those cliché statements that would point out that how feared and deadly he is, or perhaps open with a heartfelt memory from his childhood. Billy is a big kidder so maybe throw in a joke to highlight that side to him or highlight the love he has for his family, all tempting all valid but would that really grasp the embodiment that is Billy? I didn't think so, so I eventually decided to use a line that Billy has used on numerous occasions when describing himself to those willing to listen and that is simply...

If you're looking for a nice guy, you're looking in the wrong place! I'm [Billy] a horrible cunt most of the time and I get angry quickly but I can admit it!

William Martindale

It can't be easy being the son of a known fighter, Billy's Dad, Lew Yates, has had most of his life documented in publication already. The book, 'Wild Thing – the true story of Britain's rightful Guv'nor' told his story regarding his quest to fight the highly respected unlicensed fighter Roy Shaw, his sad and trouble personal life and his views on the situations that arose throughout the years. At 5ft 9" and 18 stone, Lew casted a big shadow and living under the protection of it may have been the smart move to make in life but Billy say's he tried to steer clear of trading in on his name and reputation by being my own man, despite taking the same fake identity of saying his name was 'Yates' when moving down to London, an area where Lew Yates was feared and respected and started his life amongst those that are just whispers to the common person. Either way, making that mark of being your own man meant of course making his own mistakes, mistakes that cost his upbringing dearly and it is only now that he can lay them to rest and air the truth behind them all.

William Martindale entered the world fighting; it must have been the genes he had inherited from his Dad, because it was a touch and go situation for his mother, Jean and him during his birth. Complications arose that day in the living room of his parents new home back in July 1973 that almost claimed both their lives, even then he had to out run death, if he knew then that he would be spending his young adult life running from what could have been, perhaps he would have gave up the chase and let nature take its course, but like I said, he inherited his Dad's genes and his perseverance to keep on fighting.

My dad was constantly training, some of my first memories of dad was punching his white canvas bloodstained punch bag and running miles, lifting weights and his formidable explosive temper, chasing people and coming home from working the doors with other peoples blood on him

William Martindale

Billy's mother Jean holding Glynn and Joanne

Billy standing outside the house he was born in with his own daughter, Lilly.

My son Billy Martindale, from the day he was born he had the devilment in him. I remember my first wife jean coming back one day from shopping she had a little 3 year old Billy with her on the bus. Well Billy being Billy was running all over the bus jumping up and down on the seats shouting and screaming, this man who obviously started to get the hump said something to jean and in reply to this little Billy jumped on the seat and started shaking his fist and the passenger screaming at him, even at that age he was not frightened at all and this was the shape of things to come.

Lew `wild thing` Yates

Lew in 1981 – weighing 19st

Billy's first, real memory of the woman who nearly lost her life to have him come into the world was not of her face, her perfumed scent etc but the feeling of her not being there. She would leave the family with a neighbour or at times just Billy, the family being Billy's older brother Glynn (9) and his sister Joanne (8) whilst she used to go out all the time whilst his Dad was away working the nightclub doors in London. Work was scarce back then in the neighbouring villages so his Dad would travel down to London and work as a bouncer for most of the week because the wages he could earn could more than cover the cost of all their bills in a fraction of the working time he would have had to put in by staying local. Back in the day you could earn a good living without all this bollocks of being licensed, paying tax and giving you're your home details to the local councils.

Needless to say, as children they couldn't grasp the notion that Mum was meeting another man every time she left the family home. She had met someone else and to be honest, Billy can look back now and not really blame her for falling for someone else and wanting out of an unhappy relationship with a husband that was never around whilst bringing up 3 kids. But that doesn't mean he excused her actions or behaviour when it came to leaving his siblings alone at times because she needed to escape reality and spend time with her mystery man. Who leaves their young children alone in a house for the sake of adult time? That time period of 1976 a three year old was killed in Leeds by Child killer Mark Roundtree, Donald Neilson – The Black Panther was on trial for killing Heiress, 17 year old Leslie Downing. So letting an 8 & 9 year old fend for themselves just because they should have been in bed is not the right attitude as a parent.

One night Billy's Dad phoned home to tell his waiting spouse that he was coming home earlier than expected due to a conflict of work schedules at the club he was working at only to have the phone ring off the hook due to no adult being around to answer it. My Dad just jumped in his car and drove back up to their home, believing that they would be back from wherever their mother had taken them to that evening and be glad to see him home. Of course, several hours later when he finally reached home, his Mum had still not returned from her rendezvous and Lew came in to find his eldest children in their rooms. Billy was round the babysitter's house (the actual events of that traumatic and rainy night for Lew features in his biography).

Needless to say he went mad; he phoned all of his wife's friends trying to locate her whereabouts but to no avail. She did get word though of Lew's early return and proceeded to stay away from her home and children for a few days whilst waiting for the situation to die down. Eventually though she left all the family for a new life with her new man but bill's still needed to be paid and Lew still needed to work… even more so because now he had to pay for child minders whilst out earning a wage, a case of being dammed if you do and dammed if you don't.

I was raised in a peaceful little part of Lancashire called Rossendale Valley; our stone cottage was ideally placed amongst the rolling hills where the grime and crime of urban areas were non-existent. I swear that Julie Andrews was just one second away from strolling into plain view singing about how the hills were alive with the sound of music. It was an idyllic setting for a beautiful family home but if the truth be told, my parents relationship was forever rocky, due mainly to my Dad's possessive nature, which was more than evident where my Mum was concerned. I wouldn't say he was a jealous man but he was protective, a little too protective but as the years rolled on, justified. But you have to understand that it was not a politically correct environment with women's rights and all that in them days. That's just how it was.

William Martindale

The opportunity for Lew to rack up some hours down in London arose and in pure desperation he asked Billy's grandparents, if they would let the kids stay with them for a few days. Now remember these are their grandparents, they are their grandchildren and no matter how they felt about his Dad or the nomadic life he presented to their young and impressionable daughter, the children were still innocent pawns in an adult's game of life. They agreed and Lew, albeit weary of might happen in his absence, set out on his journey back down to London to earn the money needed to support his family. Now instead of looking after the children and enjoying the fact they have their grandchildren to themselves for a few days, they had all three of them admitted to a children's home… worse still, they agreed to have the siblings split up.

Billy's sister Joanne was sent to a different care home to his brother Glynn and him. Billy can look back on it all now and realise that with such heartless parents like that to guide her, you can almost understand why his Mum's own school of thought on doing right by her children and always providing a mother's love no matter what was never apparent. Those few nights they stayed there Billy felt extremely lonely, his Mum had left them and he thought his Dad had too, his sister wasn't around and Billy used to cry himself to sleep every night wanting someone to come and collects them and make them all a whole family again. The only thing that kept Billy sane was a toy car he constantly played with, it was an old die cast of the car from the TV series, 'Kojak' starring Telly Savalas. The one with the little plastic figure leaning out of the car window with a gun in its hand, it was new so the gold colouring was all shiny and he played with it all day every day driving it around the patio area in the garden of the children's home.

Playing car's with his big brother was the only way he could get through the day and he would amerce himself into this fantasy realm of cops and robbers praying for the hours to fly by so a another day would be over. That was until he heard the booming sound of his Dad's voice echo through the building as he argued with the carers. The argument went from verbal to physical as the carers feebly attempted to stop Lew from collecting his boy's up and taking them back to their own home.

I remember seeing my Dad charge through the care house like a bull in a china shop, allowing nothing and no one stop him from reaching his children, I felt truly saved that day.

William Martindale

When they got outside, they could see Joanne already sitting in the clapped out old banger his Dad had bought off his car dealing mate, Neville Sheen for £300. It was an old 110 Wolsey with a dodgy tax disc and a roof rack full of furniture. They weren't going back to their little idyllic stone cottage in the land of sugar and spice with Julie Andrews voice ever present in the grassy hills but down to the smoke of London. They were a family again and this time Lew wasn't taking any chances, he was keeping them all a lot closer to him and his work. They were all squashed up in the car as Lew had filled it with as much of their stuff that he could. Billy clung tight to his Dad's arm has he drove, he was perched on the car's central arm rest and wouldn't let go, although Lew may of felt it hindered his ability to drive comfortably, he never told Billy to get off or moaned about the dribble and tears that he must have soaked his shoulder with, I think like the rest of them, he was happy to be all together again. The Martindale's set off down the motorway towards their new home in Windsor Road, Forest Gate, which is in the East End of London where Billy's pet Ferret, Sniffer was waiting for him. Lew had sorted out a flat for all of them to stay in, all of them except their Mum of course, she was out of their lives and the move to London was for a fresh start for all of them.

I was only 3; I remember that I never let my dad out of my sight as I thought he was going to leave me as well. I was out of nappies before mum left but after she left I pissed the bed every night, I couldn't sleep alone and always had to sleep on my dad's chest on the sofa and I would wet him every night. I was 3 and it damaged me so much, dad couldn't even go to the toilet without me by his side, he had to leave the door open and even in the day for years I would have to go everywhere with him, and I mean everywhere....

William Martindale

Windsor Road, Forest Gate, London

Billy used to think about her on occasion, even does so today but now being a parent himself, he just cannot understand how she could have abandoned them so easily, he can never see himself walking away from his kids. The pinnacle of all those memories has to be after months of Lew trying to track down his estranged wife, he finally caught up with her and asked for a civil meeting to discuss their future and the kids. Lew took a 3 year old Billy along to see the mother he had been pining for only to have her reject him.

He ran to her, arms wide open and Jean just turned her back on her youngest child and jumped on the first bus that came along. Abandonment issues were never more so engrained in Billy as at that moment, these issues, I am sure, are the main reasons for the Jekyll and Hyde behaviour that Billy sports now in his later life. Plus trust is something that seems to be hard for Billy to accept or believe in new people that enter his domain, as I am living proof of that.

For a woman, I would have thought that would have been harder. The maternal instinct and bond that they have far exceeds what the father because of the nine months of carrying and suffering they go through, yet she gave up on us as easy as changing a job and to this day, I just don't get it.

William Martindale

The flat they moved to was a purpose built place within an old Victorian house with a granny annex on the side. It had a big communal garden with a pear tree at the end of it, Billy used to love climbing that tree and hide amongst its foliage in the summer months. We seemed to have the run of the garden as the other people that shared the converted house were reaching retirement age and the last thing they wanted to do was be surrounded by noisy kids as they sat in the sun. This was back in 1976 and Billy's ever protective father kept a very close eye on all of them over the years.

Billy and his best friend Max, the Bull Terrier.
"I used to dress him up in clothes and goggles"

Moving to Forest Gate was sad but exciting, wall to wall ferrets, my dogs, an English Bull Terrier called Max

25

and a Staff cross English called Bruno, pet magpie's and Mad Ginger, our villain cat. Dad never really liked cats but Ginger was a rough tough cat, so he fit right in.

William Martindale

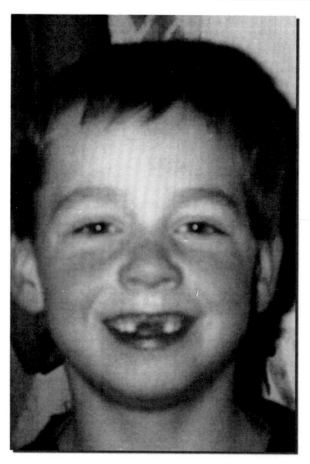

Billy aged 7

Although Billy was enrolled in school in 1978, he never really played outside of their home until he was about 8 years old. Billy had made friends in school and was always asked to go to the park etc but his Dad kept him close by, although it was thought that by the time Billy had reached 8 he had had enough of him and was grateful that he wanted to explore more than the pear tree and communal garden.

Billy could remember one time whilst Lew was outside working on the car, he was riding his bike up and down the street and Billy caught the attention of a woman who lived up the road to them. Billy was practising his wheelies or something on her little forecourt, whatever he was doing; she didn't like it and started shouting abuse at him.

"Fuck off you little bastard, you ride that bike here again, I'll cut your fucking head off, you little cunt"

nice language for an adult to shout at a minor, even more shocking was hearing it coming out of the mouth of such a delicate flower, perhaps she had missed lady etiquette 101 when the class was in session but whatever her reason to be so fouled mouthed didn't excuse the fact that Billy was only 8 years old and shouting such obscenities was well out of order. Something his Dad came over to point out to her, he had heard the commotion and told the lady to watch her mouth around his kid. Not being fazed by his size or intimidating presence she replied to his request.

"You big useless bastard, my old man will fucking have you later"

Her high pitched screech almost blew out their ear drums. Lew looked her dead in the eye and said.

"Send your old man round then. I'll be in until quarter to nine, but warn him, if he's dumb enough to come a knocking don't expect him home"

And with that he told me to get home as he followed me in. My Dad went about his business as usual, every now and then looking out the window to see if the husband of medusa was going to be brave enough to come round.

Dad was my hero, I was so proud of my big Dad, a massive animal protector, like a bear defending its cub's, you fucked with his family and he will kill you.

William Martindale

By this time in their lives, Lew had met and settled down with a woman called Margret. She was the sister of the children's old babysitter, Theresa, who looked after them when they first came down to London whilst Lew worked. Margret was a very quiet woman, a 'butter wouldn't melt in her mouth' kind of person. She cared for Lew and he cared for her and they seemed to be living the dream even with a flat full of kids.

Margaret was at first our babysitter and dad started seeing her when I was about 9. at first I got on great with her she was happy living with us in forest gat , she was like an older sister, then she fell pregnant with my younger brother Lewis and things changed for me. I was pushed out by her, and as soon as she had her own child she grew cold toward me.

William Martindale

He told Margret not to answer the door if anyone knocked once he had left and to either call him or the police if this avenging husband showed up. Lew left for work, the kids all went to bed and no more came about it.

That was until 3am when Billy heard an almighty scream come from outside his bedroom window. He peaked outside and had to rub his eyes, not because of the sleepiness in them but he couldn't believe the spectacle he was witnessing happen out on the pavement. The mouthy woman from earlier was hanging off Lew's back, wailing like a banshee, whilst trying to hit him with her shoe as his Dad was hitting her husband. Lew stood upright and threw her off him; she sailed through the air before hitting the ground that was at the bottom of the brick wall she had just gone over. All Billy could see then was a silhouette of his Dad literally dancing on someone on the ground in front of him, the body was lifeless and Billy thought that his Dad had killed him, so did the bruised wife because she was screaming at Lew to stop when out of nowhere came a transit van that she flagged down and begged the driver to call the police. The driver sped off down the road, by now Joanne and Glynn had their noses pressed up against the window too, as did half the street, whether or not the van driver did call the police, they turned up with sirens bellowing and lights flashing. A WPC approached Lew and told him to stop, which he did, it was then that Billy saw all the blood coming out of his Dad's head. Of course, Billy only saw what took place from the moment the wife started screaming and not what had caused this vicious reaction from his Dad. Lew was arrested and charged with a section 18, wounding with intent but was acquitted when it went to court as it was seen as a case of self defence.

Years later Billy asked his Dad about that night and he gave him this version of events. Lew had just pulled up after a night of working the door; he was getting out of the car when he was struck with a metal bar from behind, a typical Judas and cowardly attack. The husband had plotted himself up and had been waiting for him to return home for almost an hour, he was going in with a second swing of the metal bar when Lew punched him in the face, as he fell backwards the metal bar still caught him on the side of his face. From that point it was all over, Lew head-butted him several times before forcing the guy's head repeatedly in to the pavement slabs. As his assailant lay motionless, Lew bent down over him and started to squeeze his head. It was at that point as Lew was about to stand up that the wife attacked him from behind and let out her war cry. All this over a kid riding his bike, it makes you wonder what kind of society we live in really, doesn't it.

Dad said fighting a guy who cowardly attacked him with an iron bar was one thing but having that mouthy cunt jumping on his back and fucking screaming like she was at a rodeo just wasn't on, that was just taking the piss out of him.

William Martindale

CHAPTER 2

Lew was that kind of person, he was forever solving neighbourhood disputes with his concept of justice, from whipping people with their own car radio aerial's to beating them to near death with his bare hands, Lew laid down violent street justice plain and simple.

Another time was when young Joanne was playing with an Asian kid from up the road. This lad had been going to Karate lessons for a while and whether it was down to him showing off or whatever, he did a high roundhouse kick to her. He had no intention of hitting her, he was meant to be demonstrating how close he can get to someone without connecting but he obviously needed a few more lessons because he caught her on the side of his head. Naturally, Joanne ran back home, crying her eyes out so Lew waited in hiding for the lad behind their neighbour Stan's car. As their roads answer to Bruce Lee walked past, Lew jumped up from behind the green Austin Princess car, grabbed hold of him and literally shock him like a rag doll before throwing on to the bonnet of Stan's motor.

It should be pointed out that Stan was actually in his car installing a new car stereo at the time and despite his car was getting dented by Lew throwing the Karate kid around, never looked up once to witness the commotion, I guess some things are best left unseen. As for the Asian lad, he sobbed an apology for hurting Joanne and that was his lesson learned, Lew really shock him up, the kid was just lucky he was still a teenager and not a man because I dread to think what Lew would have done to him then.

Billy aged 8

My Dad was like that, he was and still is a very intimidating figure with an even more intimidating presence and to us kids he was the bogey man. I'm not saying he abused us, beat us etc far from it but we never wanted the possibility to arise that he may smack us with those shovel like hands of his. Not that my brother or sister had to really worry about that, they were good as gold all the time, I'm not sure where I went wrong but all their naughtiness must have been given to me in exchange for rational thinking and good looks lol Looking back on it now it was evident that I am more like my Dad even from that young age than either of us would like to admit and I think that became the root of the problems that would later bloom between us.

William Martindale

Billy had a short attention span which was ironic for a kid always seeking attention, so he wasn't really applying himself in School. He fell behind on his school work and ended up having to spend time with a counsellor, exploring his feelings and explain what was happening at home. Billy felt like he was being set up to be taken away again so just said that everything was fine. When asked why he was falling behind he explained that he was bored and the subjects were not something he had an interest in, teach him about something he liked and he would show you a pupil who could excel but if it didn't capture his interest then he just switched off. Although the counsellor was there to try and help, it didn't change the fact that Billy was goofing off in school and adding to the problems that were weighing down on his Dad's broad shoulders.

The split from my Mum and the lifestyle and work conditions my Dad was in caused him to go into a bout of depression that he tried to cure by taking to the bottle. I used to be scared when he would come home drunk because he was like Jekyll and Hyde, you never knew if he was going to gather us all up and profess his love for us or be the grouch and keep us at arm's length. He just became very distant and being the youngest I wasn't fully aware of the grown up side to it all, I just knew that my Dad seemed to be drifting apart from us kids and I retaliated by getting into trouble through fighting, stealing etc just to get his attention. I didn't care if it was negative attention that could result in me being punished; I just wanted to get a reaction from my Dad not to make his life worse but selfishly, to make mine feel better.

William Martindale

Lew and Margret's wedding day

Billy was forever getting to fights at school which in turn spilled on to the streets on his way home. On one occasion he got into one fight with the younger brother of the Asian lad who had been shaken up by his Dad. The Asian family were followers of the Sikh religion and the Sikh's believe peace under one God but Billy was giving cause to abandon that thought.

I was on my way back from the shops with a packet of custard creams for me Dad and I bumped into him outside the house. We started to arguing and I done him over the head with the custard creams, my Dad came to the window, shouting 'Go on Billy, right hook, uppercut, lift him up son, go on, go on' I done him and pulled off his bobble turban, threw it in the bin and chased him home and smashed two of his windows....

William Martindale

Billy ran back home and banged on the front door and Lew answered it. As he stepped out, Billy ran passed him to get into the safety of their home. Upon seeing his Dad standing there in their front garden, the chasing family stopped in their tracks, they wouldn't come any closer and started shouting warnings and abuse at Billy as he sat looking out the window at them. Lew just challenged them to come closer and repeat what they were saying to his face but they wouldn't so he taunted them and verbally abused them back. Needless to say they involved the police who eventually turned up but as these were from the same station that responded on the night of Lew nearly killing the banshee's husband, they too were not in a rush to come any closer than they had to.

...Then the police came to question me but with two van loads as they knew of Dad and what he was like, they stayed on the pavement and wouldn't come to the door.

William Martindale

Billy got a wrap on the knuckles from the police and that was it, not bad for his first encounter with the law, Lew kept a very watchful eye over the proceedings and wouldn't allow the coppers to come any closer than the garden wall.

Having such a scary Dad had its perks for Billy but he got an earful off him once he came back inside, but it did provide that attention that Billy was sorely seeking but at the cost of someone else's home and life being affected.

Billy's next cry for attention was sought by running away from home, as with any youngster who pulls a move like this, Billy thought he had it all worked out but his latest attempt to steal some emotional connection away from his brother and sister didn't have the devastating impact he was hoping for.

Me and my mate Paul Copping planned to run away from home and we left with a couple of quid and a bag of food and planned to live in the old bomb shelter over Wansted flats opposite Manor Park station, but dad found us 3 hours later

William Martindale

Billy's adventurous nature and need for emotional recognition was further aided when he broke into a car repairs garage with his pal, Eddy Woodman, which was only one road over from where Billy lived, not shitting on your own doorstep wasn't a rule he had yet been enlightened on. The car's were all waiting to be collected or to be M.O.T'd, so the keys were all there for the taking, the mischievous tykes jumped into a MK3 Ford Cortina and started her up. Billy had basic working knowledge of how to drive, his Dad was an avid mechanic and he had watched over his shoulder for years but that didn't change the fact both Eddy and himself were ten.

Billy pushed down on the clutch pedal to put her into gear, Eddy released the hand brake and Billy then hit the accelerator pedal without having a clear view of what was in front of them. The car shot off, Eddy screamed for Billy to push down on the brake but with his screaming and the pure fear of being inside a runaway vehicle, Billy panicked and pushed down even harder on the accelerator. The car tore off and careered through the adjoining garden fence of the house next door, the high pitched sound of the car needing to have its gears changed added to the situation that was now truly out of control.

From one garden to another, the car ploughed through the wooden fencing until it hit a fish pond, the car dipped and was now stuck, the pair of them were screaming out of terror, adrenaline was pumping through their tiny veins and Billy was still pushing down on the accelerator pedal.

The engine that was now partly covered in water started to overheat and steam came up from under the bashed up bonnet as the wheels were still spinning at high speed and caused the water and the fish from the pond to be forced up and sprayed onto the messed up lawn.

Of course their commotion had woken up the occupants from the two houses they had just driven through and their neighbours. The old lady that owned the house with the fish pond was yelling at the top of her voice, as she approached them in the car, she peered through the window still yelling which in turn made the boys scream even louder and finally they got the idea to bolt for it. They opened the driver's door, splashed into the half empty pond and took off over the next garden fence and so on.

They could hear police sirens wailing in the distance as they made their way back to Eddy's house, his Mum answered the door, looking down at them with tear marks down their angelic faces, pond soaked trousers and a shortness of breath with police cars in the background.

That got both of them more attention than either of them wanted.

Although I was happy to get the interest from my father, I was only giving him the excuse to be angry with me and after a while I felt that being angry was acceptable and with anger came the violence. I was going to school in a very angry and violent mood and soon found myself getting into trouble with the Headmaster because I was always fighting. I started to get a little reputation in the playground and would get other kids wanting to fight me and such, then it became groups of kids and when that started I had a pal who was nicknamed 'Ginger John' came stand with me to take on all comers. Eventually our folks were summoned in by the Headmaster to discuss our behaviour and suitable punishment, but my Dad being the

37

kind of man he was just told the Headmaster to shut up and not even think about punishing his son or he may have to physically punish the Headmaster, needless to say my card was sincerely marked from that that day forth by both the school and my Dad. Not to mention the fact that Tom's parents decided I was a bad influence on their son and were never happy at the prospect that we were friends.

William Martindale

Bovver Boy Billy, aged 9 – DM's, braces and a Muscle t-shirt

CHAPTER 3

The Martindale's were big fans of animals and pets in their household, the latest one was a Staffordshire bull terrier, he was an approachable dog, was good with kids but the addition of him along with the other pets they kept meant that the other families that were part of the communal garden never ventured into it, they had the whole area to themselves. One afternoon Ginger John, a school friend of Billy's came round and Billy started teasing their dog to attack him, he started barking at John and John was telling Billy to cut it out who was standing there laughing when all of a sudden the dog got loose of his grip and went for John. John covered up the best he could, raising his arms to protect his face which caused him to lose his balance as the dog jumped up on to him. With John now on the ground, still covering his face the dog bit into John's overflowing Ginger hair and started to pull him around the garden. Rather than acting with urgency, Billy just stood and watched the commotion, laughing at the situation, a little of it was out of fear that his mate was about to be ripped apart by his dog when Lew came out to the garden. He went fucking mad, he shouted at the dog to release John, whilst shouting at Billy for standing there laughing rather than helping, he grabbed the dog that let go of John straight away, poor John was crying, it was a complete mess, and that's when Billy realised that he felt really bad for what he made happen to his pal, the same guy that had his back in school.

John eventually forgave Billy but understandably never wanted to be in the same room as the dog again, not that Billy would blame him but he knew that by involving the family pets in his cries for attention, he had crossed a line and his Dad let Billy know it in no uncertain terms. He made it clear that stunts like that could result in them having to have the dog put to sleep if John's parents took the matter further and he was declared as being dangerous. As usual Billy just didn't think of the consequences that came with his actions but he did learn what really pushed his Dad's buttons and that was something he did have an interest in.

Ginger John Trebess, he was one of my best pals from junior school, we played together all the time. He lived on Capel Rd, Forest Gate opposite Wanstead flats. I miss him, he was a good friend last I heard he and his two brothers were in the police force.

William Martindale

To help Billy change his ways in school, his teacher played on the fact that he was comfortable around animals and so he was given the responsibility to take home the class gerbils and look after during half term. They were both males and were kept in separate cages, normally two children would get the honour of looking after them but the teacher thought if Billy had to take twice as much care and responsibility it may teach him something worthwhile that could aid him to become a more sensible and less violent child. Billy got home with both the cages and put them in his room, for the first two days he enjoyed looking after them but of course you have to clean out their cages so Billy thought why not have them both share one cage and therefore he would only have one cage to clean. It didn't matter that they were both males, Billy shared a room with another male and they get on, what's the worst that could happen? What indeed, keeping in kind this rationale was coming from someone who knew about animals. Billy placed both Gerbils into one cage, left some food and water for them and left them alone as he went off to play in the garden. When he came back in to check on them, they were both okay and happily sharing the space when out of nowhere one bites the other one, causing them to fight, their squeaky squeals were deafening as they went at each other. This gladiatorial bout went on for about ten minutes, they would stop every now and then when a real good scratch or bite was given but it ended the same way as those who fought in the coliseum and that was with one alive and the other one dead. Billy was never allowed to look after school pets again.

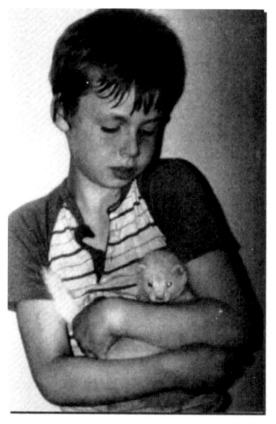

Billy aged 9 holding a ferret

I love all animals, more than people, I love nature, the countryside, and I always wanted to work for the RSPCA as a kid.

Billy Martindale

Another time Billy took in one of his ferret's for a show and tell session, in total he had about 40 ferrets and pole cats, rabbits, cats, dogs etc in their garden, you can imagine what kind of stench came from them, the kid's weren't the best liked neighbours for obvious reasons. Billy's teacher at that time was Mr. Jack, a big built bloke due to his passion for playing rugby, who sported a woolly beard and the ferret he took in reflected that by being the biggest blonde haired ferret from the bunch who also had an overly hairy chin and resembled Mr. Jack to a tee. The other children gathered round as Billy presented it to them, there wasn't that many city kids had seen a ferret up close let alone a big monster, Mr. Jack look-a-like that this one was. Ferrets are a Northerner's chosen pet and so was a rarity for his classmates from down South, in the smoky depths of East London to get a chance to see and pet. Mr. Jack came over and seemed just as bemused as the children were and dived in to pick the ferret up and to hold.

The ferret started to lick and nibble on Mr. Jack's beard much to the delight to the children that were watching Mr. Jack let the ferret carrying on licking his face as it sniffed around his hair until the ferret reached Mr, Jack's ear. Mr. Jack's earlobe quivered with the sensation of the ferret sniffing around his ear, which in turn caught the attention of the ferret, which then sank his teeth into it making Mr. Jack yell in pain, he let go of the ferret that was now hanging from his ear like a Mr. T feather earring. The children were all laughing at the ferret that was now digging his claws into Mr. Jack's neck to get the leverage to tear off the earlobe that it was attached to. In hindsight it might have proved useful for Billy to have fed the ferret before bringing him into school but like the Gerbil situation, Billy couldn't see what could go wrong.

Billy aged 10 – outside his house in Windsor Rd, Forest Gate.
His Dad's cars on the drive – a Viva, Toledo and a Jag.

Billy was only ten years of age and he had already caught the attention of the police, the school authorities and his neighbours. At a time when any rightful thinking adolescent would rethink their actions and live with the attention that they so dearly sought had been obtained and take the time to simmer down and stop putting unnecessary pressure on those that loved them despite recent actions but no, Billy had to take it further. His last attempt to run away from home had failed miserably but that didn't stop him from packing a few things up and walking to Manor Park, a couple of miles away and stayed in the City of London Cemetery. He managed to survive for two days before being caught and his Dad was called to collect him, Lew was furious more through worry than anything else but as with everything else Billy pondered on he just didn't understand what the outcome could possibly be a wrong one. He couldn't comprehend that the consequences would be more than a raised voice or even a spanked backside from his Dad, he didn't factor in that social services could get involved and take him away from a lone parent, who couldn't control him, kids never can understand the penalty of their own, selfish, unruly actions. Billy was fortunate that his little stunt didn't end with such an outcome but some aren't and their plans backfire very quickly, the same goes for when you break the law to get noticed, yet another bright idea from Billy to get his Dad's interest.

It is safe to assume that Billy was a slow learner when it came to that age old rule of not shitting on your own doorstep; previous misadventures hadn't obviously sank in because his next bright idea involved a box of matches and a caravan, parked on the forecourt of his next door neighbour.

Me and Neil Kerr were playing with some matches and lit the tarp that covered the caravan alight. We thought we had put it out and so we walked off, 30 minutes later we heard sirens and saw the smoke... oops

William Martindale

My old friend, Neil Kerr

I just got in contact with my old friend from when I was 9, his name is Neil Kerr we were good pals years ago, and we burnt the caravan down accidentally. I just found out he's gay. I don't care what he is, he's still my pal. We were little bastards when we were kids, we were skin heads and nail gave me my very first pair of oxblood Dr. Martins, we were all in dm's and Fred Perry t-shirts. Neil realised he was gay at 12, after I had moved away, we just spent an hour on the phone and he tells me he got married to his hubby a year ago after being together for 8 years. Neil is a successful property developer. He was amazed that I had had the life of crime and if he is acceptant of my life, I'm acceptant of his, we were the same as children. He's a great guy still; I wish him all the best in all he does.

William Martindale

Yet another lucky escape befell Billy who avoided the matter being taken further. Billy was now getting into loads of fights at school, demonstrating a very bullish behaviour and a short fuse due to frustration wanting to be like his Dad. No respect for those around him, this was proven by incidents like throwing his chips on people whilst riding the bus, letting off stink bombs etc and would constantly get his straight laced brother Glynn in to trouble by starting trouble with other kids and then blaming it on to his brother.

Where do I start? When he was a kid, I sometimes wished that there was a special big wooden box in the corner where we could contain him with just a few holes in it (only a few). To say his hyperactivity was a distraction is an understatement. He seemed to have no boundaries as he would dance about in front of the TV, flicking his nasty little winky about the place, cause he wasn't getting the attention that he obviously thought he deserved. My mates would call round and it wasn't long before he was on their case. From the window I would see him descend on them

45

with some kind of verbal assault or otherwise, and then it had almost become a tradition/reflex action to take off after him and beat him with whatever was to hand. He obviously enjoyed it because he kept coming back for more (strange I know). He also nearly killed the little old man from next door by taking off on his BMX from a ramshackle ramp he made, and practically landed on top of him. I think the old guy was religious, so I guess he was praying to, and thanking whoever that night for getting off so lightly. Fortunately he improved (like he could get any worse) in many ways. He has always been entertaining, once turning up on my door-step dressed as a giant chicken.

I'm not sure to this day what the exactly the motivation to do such a thing was, but it brightened my day both spiritually and literally, as it was a very bright yellow. He has always supported me when I was in difficulty and helped me without hesitation, and so I know that I can rely on him when push comes to shove. He has done some bad stuff of course, but hey, that's what this book pretty much covers anyway and let's face it, crime and corruption happens at all levels, it's only the poorer end of the scale that seems to be highlighted with any regularity. I wish him all the best and love him as a brother should.

Glynn Martindale

Lew knew that Billy needed structure and discipline and enrolled him into the one thing that Lew knew and respected what a person could get out of it if you put in the effort and that was boxing. Billy, although shown many a trick and tip from his formable father, was signed up to the Little Eye Boxing Club if to at least burn up his energy and take a bit of wind out of his sails. He had no such luck.

Billy sent to Little Eye Boxing Club at age 10

Little eye boxing club, I boxed there with Frankie from Salisbury Jnr school. Dad taught me more than any trainer could. Dad taught me to fight dirty, head butts, fingers in eyes, biting and how to throw a cracking right hand. To this day I still have not lost my exceptional hand and eye co-ordination.

William Martindale

Whilst all the attempts to curb Billy's hyperactive exploits were in full swing, Lew still had to contend with his own lifestyle of working the doors of London nightclubs and it was after a failed attempt on his life because of his profession that it was decided to get out of the dangerous urban attractions and start life over again as a family in a quieter area, a more rural environment, it was decided that Manea, Cambridgeshire was where the Martindale's would set up shop and start to let the good times roll.

CHAPTER 4

Manea was a far cry from the hustle and bustle of London, this Fenland village sandwiched between Chatteris and March may have been just less than an hour's drive from Peterborough or Cambridge but it was a different world entirely. It has its own train station but with only one train arriving in the morning and the next one is in the evening. I wouldn't say the village was small but if I was a stand up comedian the following one-liners would be deemed appropriate:

- A "Night on the Town" takes only 11 minutes
- The phone book has only one page
- The McDonalds only has one Golden Arch
- No social events can be scheduled when the school gym floor is being varnished
- During a boxing match, both men have to sit in the same corner
- There was no town idiot - everybody had to take turns
- The Village prison is called amoeba, because it only has one cell
- Everyone knows all the news before it's published; they just read the local paper to see whether the publisher got it right
- The "road hog" in front of you on the High Rd is a farmer's combine
- The Mayor was also the police chief, town council & street sweeper
- The village Lady of the Evening stands under a flashlight
- There was no porno cinema; once a week someone left the shades up

And so on and so on and so on, you get the picture, small village, hyperactive wild child, you do the math.

To help beat the boredom, Billy continued to do what he knew before leaving Forest Gate and that was to join a boxing gym.

Even though I was in a couple of boxing clubs, what my dad taught me was so so valuable to me a lot of it was dirty but effective. I was told off a few times for using my dad's skills, and one night as my dad will tell you himself I was knocking around some of the experienced fighters at Chatteris boxing club, they gave me 18 oz gloves to wear to spar with their fighters and dad came in and went mental, threw the trainer across the floor and dragged me out but to be honest dad was disappointed with me as he said I had the ability and plenty of courage but when I got home from school I got fed up of doing 5 miles roadwork , and then pad work , floor to ceiling ball and all the other training that went with it.

Sparing with dad was tough, and that's another question I have been asked on many occasions, people have said many many times when I have turned up to row with people written about in books And other assorted rats, why I'm not bothered by these pretend cunts .... And I say.... I have grown up with the scariest man alive why the fuck should I worry about people like that? I know 100% even though I'm over weight I would bite holes in the cunt.... I'm in tune with my abilities.

William Martindale

Lew with Dave 'Boy' Green

There is a side of Billy where he is very intelligent and a quick learner so when he was in his teens I started to teach him boxing and it didn't take him long to become very good he shaped up really well he had lovely movement and was very quick, anyways I decided to take him to Chatteris boxing club where Davey boy green used to train, and straight away the coach at the club asked if Billy would spar with one of their boys yea no problem, one after the other Billy just toyed with them not one of them could give him any trouble so I thought fuck this and never took him again.

Billy would mess about too much and wouldn't train, which is a shame, because he would have been a good boxer.

Lew `wild thing` Yates

And with a new place to live came the need to attend a new school, being the new kid is one thing, being a new kid from out of the village community was another. Although Billy wasn't a true Londoner, being born in Lancashire, he had spent his childhood there and grew up with an urban experience and not a rural one; he felt left out and knew that he had to fit on if he was to enjoy this new start in life.

It was difficult for me. I found the area to be quite a clique place and I was an outsider.

William Martindale

Billy aged 11 – his first school picture whilst in Manea

Needless to say, the thought of having to go into school every day with people that didn't want to talk to him wasn't a pleasant time, so young Billy would try a number of scams, tricks and excuses not to be sent in on his Dad and Step mum Margret. Some worked but a majority didn't so Billy lay awake at night thinking of other ways to get out of going to school, one thought was to sabotage the school bus that came round to collect the kids at certain points of the village.

The coach used to collect me from outside my house; the coach driver was called Nibby and was also the landlord of the Dunn Cow pub in Christchurch, a small village not too far away from Manea. I hated school so one day I thought of a plan to get the day off school, I thought it was a good idea to get some 1" large headed felt nails and put a line of about 10 nails in the path of the school bus, so when he stopped to collect me he was bound to run over them. I stood on the side of the road waiting for the bus to come pass, as Nibby stopped the bus the tyres went over the nails and I knew that it wouldn't be long before the bus had to stop due to having flat tyres.

I boarded the bus, we did about 7 miles or so then of all places the front left tyre went flat as we was travelling along the Stone road, which the 16 foot river runs alongside. Poor old Nibby struggled to control the bus and we nearly ended up in the river, OMG I could have killed us all.... to make things worse my plan didn't work, we had to just wait for another bus , so we didn't get the day off after all lol

William Martindale

It was after that stunt that Billy really got noticed by the local children and it wasn't long after joining his new school that Billy attracted likeminded friends who liked to walk on the wild side and make the quiet village streets a little bit noisier.

Moving to Manea was weird, exciting and hard. Leaving Windsor Rd in London to a farm house in the Fens was chalk and cheese, boring at first, locals didn't except you. But when they did we made our own fun building camps, sleeping under the railway bridge in underground dens with Darren 'Nobby' Newman, Carl Dawson and Gary Loads – they were all naughty boys from Manea.

Billy Martindale

Billy, aged 11 on his BMX – Manea, Cambs

With new found friends, Billy's life in this quiet town picked up and the gang of miscreants he was now a part of got up to a number of things throughout Manea and its neighbouring villages. Many a time the local bobby, who patrolled on a bicycle between the hours of 10am and 4pm, would be bringing Billy back to his home with that 'clip round the ear' policing mentality; a 'boys will be boy's' type attitude and a 'I don't want to write up any paperwork' ethic. Billy was getting a reputation for being a bad influence; in London he would be called a cheeky sod, in the country he was on par with a young Al Capone and matters got worse when he made himself fully know at Cromwell Community College.

Billy and Mr. King outside Cromwell Community College

My head at Cromwell was a Mr. Atkins, I didn't have many dealings with him but my deputy head, Mr. Dring was a different matter. He was a tall, skinny man in a brown suit, real old fashioned teacher. He scared me, he caned me twice, his cane was the bottom half of an old fishing rod, complete with the cork handle and the rest was wrapped lovingly in black electrical tape. I don't hold grudges against my teachers as I think the kids needed it, well the kids like me did and they still do today.

When I went back to see my old school teachers recently, I thought to myself 'What nice guys they are', just goes to show you when you're a kid all the world is against you or at least seemed to be.

My P.E. teacher, Mr. Robinson and Mr. Kent were real nice people. Mr. Hunt, my science teacher, had me round the throat once as I lit the gas from the table top tap and took Paul Clarks eyebrows off lol Whhhoooofffff, it went and Mr. Robinson grabbed me and held his fist back and with a bright red face, said 'I want to punch your head in Martindale, so help me God I will...'

I would like to meet him again and buy him a beer....

William Martindale

It was here that made friends with a young Tommy Shepherd and his brothers, who would quickly become Billy's best friends.

Tommy Shepherd

Once I started school at Cromwell Community College at Chatteris, I met the Shepherd lads and the rest of their crew, Tommy, Freddy, Anh, Butt, Joe, Ken, Percy plus Lee Baxter, Scott Payne, The Beenie's and Sam Vinden. These were the local traveller boys all with a mischievous streak running through them. We got on straight away but it was Tommy who was the star above them all, he became my best friend. Freddy was a pain in the arse lol always laughing as life was a big joke but still a good kid deep down.

William Martindale

Darren 'Nobby' Newman, Billy and Freddy Shepherd

Now friends with the local travellers, Billy found a community that accepted him, especially the parents of the Shepherd boys and in turn he accepted them. His home life had not changed despite the move to start over; Margret was neglecting of him and concentrated her motherly affection towards her own offspring. So to finally find a home environment that he connected with meant a great deal to Billy.

Billy with Mr. and Mrs. Shepherd

I used to go to home to Tommy's Mum and Dad's shiny, stainless steel trailer at dinner break and home time. Rose, Tommy's Mum, was and still is so house-proud; their pace was/is immaculate. You had to take your shoes off, she had crockery and glassware everywhere, she was and is a great mother who kept an immaculate home and would kill for her boys. A real strong woman.

William Martindale

The gang was now established and in turn they used to wreak havoc in Manea and Chatteris. They were just kids trying to get their hands on some money so they would steal cars and scrap metal and do whatever they could to get a note and when that opportunity wasn't available, they would just disrupt the local community with their law breaking antics.

We'd get into fights at the village discos, we once nicked a gas forklift and stuck it in a river, another time we nicked a tractor, then burnt a haystack down after we left our fag butts near it, and of course there was the joy riding in the lorries, we would take them out and then put them back with an empty fuel tank, parking them in the same place so they wouldn't realise and just believe that they forgot to fill it up ready for their deliveries. We were always getting up to stuff like that.

William Martindale

Billy's antics weren't going unrecognised by his Dad.

Around this time he was getting more and more into trouble and one day when he was around 13 years old we were in the back garden on the farm and he started to be a bit cheeky I told him to fucking shut it but he kept it up so I lost it and he ran, at the time I had a big bag of potatoes next to the farm house door and as he jumped over the fence at the bottom of the garden I flung the biggest one I could see at him he turned and started laughing and giving me the finger as he did… bang, I got him right on the head and he went down dizzy he tried to run so I grabbed my shotgun and started to take pot shots he was running from side to side and went out of sight.

There was also another time when I was chasing Billy down the road with my rifle, then all of a sudden he was gone fuck it I couldn't believe I had lost him then all of a sudden in the middle of this big corn field I saw his head pop up to see where I was, bang I shot at him he went down I thought yes I got the little cunt but just as I was going to walk away his head popped up again at the edge of the field BASTARD I took another shot and again he went down this

59

happened another 2 times before he jumped the fence and legged it over the railway lines and disappeared.

Lew `wild thing` Yates

All this activity just brought the attention of the police to the doorstep time and time again and coupled with the strain on the home already with Margret's feelings towards Billy that it wasn't long before Billy would find himself all home alone on the weekends.

Billy aged 13 with his younger siblings Lewis and Vicky

As a teenager, my step mum was a nasty, wicked old bag who was only interested in her own kids (my step siblings, Lewis and Vicky). She would lie to my Dad and make shit up, set me up for trouble at any time she could. My Dad never heard her swear but when he worked away in London, doing the door in a club in Dagenham, she would chase me around a bit with whatever she could pick up to hit me with shouting 'You fucking little cunt, I'm gonna kill you!' and I'm trying to run whilst laughing, as it was great to get her angry as I knew I had got to her. She would never cook for me or wash my clothes, it was abuse, so I got my own back every weekend lol and eventually she couldn't cope anymore and started going down to London with my Dad leaving me alone in our house in Manea. Yeah I had won and I loved it, because that made me king of the castle on the weekends, with a long barrelled bolt action shot 4/10 shotty as company.

Dad never believed me on how wicked she and disturbed she was, until of course when they got divorced and now he knows lol most of my younger siblings despise her... the sick bitch.

William Martindale

Me and my English Mastiff, Zoe playing with one of the steel drums I shot at with the 4/10 shotgun.

So his father left him to fend for himself with a shotgun as he travelled back to London for work. He told Billy that if anyone came to the house and gave him trouble he should shoot into the air and crack them over the head with it. Billy, of course, just had fun shooting at cans and anything else he could get his hands on in the back garden.

As he grew up he became a little terror and after my first wife left he started to rebel and was always in trouble one way or the other. It got to a point where my second wife would not stay at the farm alone with him as I went down London to work, this one weekend I needed to go to work on the doors in London and Margret came with me, with the farm being so secluded and a 12 year old Billy being left on his own I gave him a 4.10 long bolt action shotgun with a handful of shells just in case of intruders, well what can I say when we returned to find Bill had been shooting up my things in the garden.

Lew `wild thing` Yates

With his new found freedom, Billy wanted and needed some extra cash to supplement his independence and so started up his own car washing business but naturally, this being Billy, the customers got a particular level of service.

I started washing cars for money, one old Yorkshire gent used to have me wash his car, and he never paid me the full amount, saying he hadn't enough change, but he would only look out of the door and say 'ok thanks', he did this every time so in the end I only washed half of the car, the half he could see from the door....

William Martindale

Needless to say that enterprise didn't last long and so Billy's attention turned to motorbikes.

We got into motorcycles, fs1e ar125 all them bikes, all my pals from school had bikes, Ian Jones another of my mates had just been treated by his mum and dad to a brand new Simpson 50 cc bike. We were out riding on those things all the time. We had all the classics, AR 50's, FS1 E's, AP 50's, RD 125, RD 350's, they got bigger and bigger.

William Martindale

Billy still as a passion for motorbikes today.

Whilst out riding one day, a fatal accident took place that highlighted that life is just too short for some.

Ian Jones died on his white Simpson 50cc at Benwick, when he was 16, he went round the corner and hit a tractor pulling a plough, it decapitated him. His head was still in his helmet when the ambulance men found it. Ian was a real good kid, he just wanted to be part of the gang.

William Martindale

Just after that incident Billy's love for bikes and for breaking the law got combined when he stole a Honda 100 cc motorcycle and headed off to clear his thoughts of the loss of one of his friends.

I got nicked for TDA of a 100cc Honda. I borrowed it and went to the coast for 2 days. I was gonna bring it back, honest.

William Martindale

There are so many incidents over the years which would be a book in itself, like the time Billy and his brother Lewis burnt the field down which blazed all night and took 6 fire engines to put it out or the time when I was telling him not to ride his Kawasaki 50er scrambler bike without a license but would he listen no, I kicked the bastard thing over and stamped on the tank after that he could only get half a gallon of petrol in it.

Lew `wild thing` Yates

Billy's time at school was reaching its end; he was 16 and wondering what his career options were so he undertook a work experience session.

I didn't do very well at school. I left in 1989 with no qualifications there was only one lesson school I was interested in and that was a separate lesson that was made up of all the bad and naughty kids, it was called wildlife, lol and the teacher was Mrs. Toombs, a little old grey haired lady. I must say I learned so much from her, she was a good old fashioned teacher, very strict and she would take no grief from any of us, and at last there was subject I was interested in. We would learn about birds, mammals, plants and wild flowers and fish. I flew through it with ease as I had a real interest in the subject.

I was not a nasty kid, I just wanted attention, all I wanted to do was make all the other kids laugh and still to this day I like to make people laugh, it fills me with energy and joy to see the affect I can have on people. When I think of how the kids are nowadays, "carrying knives" it's something I would never have considered as a kid; why the fuck would you want to take a knife to school????

As a teen, me and my old pals Darren Newman, Gary Loads, Carl Dawson, packed up all our makeshift survival kits and headed for the river Bedford or the Delph and sleep out under the stars. We'd build dens/ camps shelters, we loved it, we didn't have play stations, x boxes and all these games, we would have campfires, the open air and all the other things that go with our Ray Mears antics. We would catch and cook eels, pike and zanda, we would walk on the railway lines from Manea to Ely, stopping to set up camp in the surrounding scrub, and we would take foil and pinch potatoes from the fields and bake them on the fire. We would collect owl pellets from under the railway bridges, so when we got home we would soak them, to see what the owls had been eating, and rebuild the skeletons.

I started my work experience at the RSPB nature reserve, at Pearls Bridge, Manea; I loved it, working out in the open. I do love this small island which we live on; there are some stunning places to visit around the British Isles. I don't understand why were all in such a rush to go on holiday to Europe, when there are stunning places to visit and walk here. What's the point of going to Spain and just lying on the beach and getting pissed?

It's a shame this country which was once great has now gone to pot, the tax and all this p.c bollocks has ruined it. you can't speak your mind nowadays, it makes me sick.... we are second class citizens in our own country.... there will be wars in this country soon , you wait and see, it's disgusting that all those hundreds of thousands of young men died in two wars to keep this country great and just look at it.... All this money we give to other countries, when we have old people dying here of the cold in winter, live 8, what a lot of shit, charity starts at home I say.

Don't get me wrong it's terrible to see kids dying around the world of hunger and dirty water but we have been giving for so long and nothing changes, it's all corrupt, and we send more food. WTF we need to send them condoms not food, stop breeding. If most of your kids have died of starvation or are dying of starvation, then why are you still breeding????

William Martindale

Billy holding a zanda that he and Lew caught at Chatteris 16 foot river.

Once school was over, everything was started to go off the rails for Billy and the gang he went around with, friction within the Traveller's camp didn't help the atmosphere around the Village, especially when money started to go missing from one of the families.

Another traveller I knew, Jason Venie, stole an amount of cash from his uncle, his uncle caught him and he and Jason's father hung him by his hands and lashed him with horse whips for 40 minutes. He was in tatters, I

66

saw this for myself. Jason would then eventually be arrested for being involved in the killing of Tommy Shepherd.

William Martindale

Billy's time in Manea was coming to an end, as was his father's marriage. Home life wasn't something that could be enjoyed on any level and with the troubles happening amongst his surrogate family, Billy reckless abandonment was reaching the final straw. After being arrested for carrying an offensive weapon it became evident that Billy's luck was running out. The local police station wasn't well equipped, no computers or fax machines, everything was on paper in a filing cabinet stored in a dank storeroom.

It was in here that William Martindale's criminal career to date was stored, which was just as well because after a lorry yard went up in flames causing £250,000 of damages, William Martindale was nowhere to be found, Billy Yates however was making his way down to London.

Looking back on that time, one of Billy's biggest regrets as he left all that he knew and loved behind was never saying sorry to his Dad.

I rebelled against my Dad as a teenager, I think I hurt him by giving up boxing, he said I had something special, fast and powerful, good with either hand and super quick on my feet.

I was strong; I was bench pressing 175lb at the age of 11 and repping a full set not just the one. I was around the 9 stone mark (126 lbs) and agile like a cat, I had to be quick to get away from Dad lol.

I think I let him down; I didn't want the commitment of doing 5 miles of roadwork after school each day, then training and bag work.

I wanted money and girls, I have never said sorry for disappointing him so I'm saying it now, Sorry Dad.

William Martindale

CHAPTER 5

Alone, cold, destitute and with nothing more than a few quid in his pocket, Billy Yates reached familiar ground in London. In desperate need of a helping hand, Billy sought his first night on the run in the sanctuary of not a church but the next best thing, a 24/7 ESSO petrol station in Redbridge, which has ironically been renamed 'On the run'.

Billy outside the old ESSO petrol station that housed him for over a month when he first reached London.
Insert: Billy standing outside the back entrance

The ESSO petrol station I lived in for a month or so, The Indian man that worked the night shift let me sleep in the toilet, I was so cold at night I woke up every few hours and put the hand dryer on to stay warm and lined the floor with flattened down cardboard boxes. The Indian man had a heart of gold; he put an' out of order' sign on the door for me and fed me snacks.... I will never forget that man and his big heart, I would love to thank him personally.

Billy Yates

    With no contacts, no money and virtually no hope, Billy did what he needed to do to survive and that was the same thing that most homeless people resort to, sink to depths that they wouldn't normally choose to. Where some would knock on the back door of restaurants, pubs or clubs to offer to wash dishes etc for a little cash in hand, others would beg on the streets and then the rest would take from others by force. Billy Yates opted for the latter and progressed his criminal ways by going from robbing shops with the threat of physical violence, to using a weapon like a bat, then upping the ante by producing a knife and eventually, with money in his pocket and a street reputation that was growing, Billy made contacts that allowed him to get hold of a gun and he used that to rob a post office. With this kind of sudden surge in armed robberies, it wasn't long before Billy attracted the attention of other likeminded people from within the criminal circle and started to become part of a very violent and dangerous group that included Robert Josephs, Neil Charles, Chris Donnelly and Ray King.

I've known Bill now for 18 years, I was 27 and Bill was 17. I was doing bits and pieces, running around trying to earn a pound note, I was always looking at setting up scams or setting businesses up, there were lots of different fella's in my clique over the years but not many really understood how I was thinking, but Billy seemed to have that edge, for a youngster at 17 he was way ahead of other kids his age. Billy understood I was trying to find a way to work the system and making some decent money. Billy's face would light up when I was telling him stories and ideas, we would talk to the early hours of the morning about how we were gonna crack it and have a good life. 9-5 poxy jobs weren't exciting enough for us, I knew bill was a character and one day the world would be his stage. I see him going through his days of getting nicked and always kept his mouth shut with the gavers. We wrote to each other when I was in Maidstone and Bill was in Pentonville. Billy always wanted to learn, I thank Bill for putting some of my times with him in his book and wish him and his family, a happy and healthy life, love ya like a brother Bill.

Ray King

Billy with Ray King

This is one man I have the most respect for, he has the heart and confidence of a lion, his name is Ray Ogwood or King, he uses both names so many of you will know him as either. I have been good pals with Ray now for 18 years, he's also one of the most intelligent men you will ever meet, I look at Ray like an older brother, I learnt so so much from Ray it's unbelievable, he took me under his wing when , after I got out of living in the petrol station in Redbridge. I robbed a puff dealer on Tiptree Cresant in Clayhall, Barkingside, I think I netted a lousy 900 quid, but that was enough to get me a deposit on a bedsit in Cowley Rd, Gants Hill, and ray lived there as well. His room was the front and the biggest in the house, and was full of brand new washing machines and TVs lol Ray loved to trade, buy and sell, if there was a pound note Ray was there, a mind as sharp as a razor, his body language you could never read as it was far too fast and still is, his business mind is second to none. I learnt most of what I know now from this man, he's well respected for his no nonsense approach to fools , and weeds them out within a 5 minute conversation, his quick temper has let him down in the past and was diagnosed a paranoid schizophrenic and can turn at the drop of a hat. I must admit he gave me a black eye when I was 17, lol no doubt I deserved it, then a week later we were pals again, I loved the fast life I lived with Ray and I did live with him and work with him for a couple of years. Rays life was soon looking good he managed to get 4 mortgages up and running at the beginning of 1990 and that as we know was the time to buy houses, he was buzzing, proper having it off, we were clubbing, pubbing around Ilford and the West End of London, life was good and Ray and me were earning, I was about 10 stone wet through when I worked for Ray, and Ray was a muscularly 12 stone man only about 5"7/8, he was once British judo champion and 5th in Europe as a youngster and was set for the Olympics, but woman, drinking and fighting in the street destroyed Rays judo days, now Ray wanted money, Ray did at one time dabble in moving the odd lump of resin around, and was meeting a fella at Fairlop Waters.

One evening and I think he had a kilo in a holdall, Ray being Ray had a couple of drinks whilst he was waiting and decided to have a little dance fucking about with a couple of birds in there, when a butterfly knife dropped onto the floor from his pocket, with this someone has told the two head doormen, two brothers, I know them but am not going to mention names, even though I didn't like what they did, as my dad is pals with them and that's the only reason.... anyway they asked Ray to go into the office with them so he did, when they asked to look in Rays bag, Ray told them to 'fuck themselves' and there was a bit of a scuffle, when they saw what was in the bag, they gave Ray a choice, either walk out here now and leave the bag or we call the police, but Ray being Ray told them to 'fuck off'. Ray said 'that belongs to a bigger man than me or you, so ring the fucking police'. a couple of minutes went by and Ray saw the blue lights coming down the road and again the doormen said look here they come, Ray gave them bollocks and was arrested and jailed, that's how loyal Ray is he would rather get nicked and do a bird than try to explain who the owner of the puff was... if that was me I would of just sent him on his way.... Ray then later lost his temper with his mortgage man one day and threatened to kill him and left the message on his answer machine, the police and courts knowing Ray was a paranoid skitso with a violent criminal past, wanted to take no chances and 5 days later Ray was arrested and jailed for 5 years for threats to kill, so that one call lost him his houses, his booming sales in sports gear which I was helping him with and everything else, he let his mates or so called mates the Cramler's look after all his sports goods and other bits and bobs whilst he was away but they sold the lot and had no money for him when he got out.

whilst Ray was in prison, I was working on drug dealers again with Rob, Chris, and Neil, when Ray came out I went back to work with him again, and again I went on my own merry way and soon found out Ray had got 8 years for something I can't mention as he still wants to legally deal with for some compo, if he was found guilty of the more serious charge he would have got 16 years, so he had a touch. He was proper set up, I was in Pentonville when I found out Ray was in Maidstone, at the same time as Reg Kray, we would write to each other and have a laugh about the old times. When I was first released from Pentonville on judge and chambers bail, before I skipped

73

bail and went to Spain and Miami, I visited Ray twice in Maidstone, the castle on the island, I took him in some money and said goodbye and told him I was not returning to court, and leaving the country.

Ray has calmed down a fair bit now but his business brain is still second to none, I sold him a van not long ago and he took me to his lock up and threw in some quality 1930's doors with the deal, he's just like Delboy lol he's good friends with the Hunts and Dave Davis, he's well respected, I love Ray still to this day and please look out for Rays book.... What an amazing life that man's had.

Billy Yates

Rob Josephs and Billy

I met Rob Josephs after he was released from prison for a murder he didn't commit. He lived in Harcourt Ave, Manor Park and we earned loads of money and respect. Rob, like me, can be the nicest person in the world but has a very dark side. we lived in an evil, dark world of guns, stabbings, robberies, and hired bone breakers that I can't talk any more in detail about those activities, for Rob's and my sake. When we meet up now we talk about

74

things we did and laughed about them and thought if only friends we have now could know what we had done, all these little chav's who think they're bad boys, listening to Eminem and 50 cent CD's wouldn't last a fucking day in our world… it was a dark period in both our lives.

Billy Yates

Billy and Rob extorted ill gotten money from over 20 drug dealers. Rob was convicted of a murder at Havelock's pub in Ilford and served 4 years before he was released after the police found the real killer.

Chris and Billy

Me and Chris Donnelly, Chris and his dad were jailed years ago for cutting a nonce with a Stanley blade across his back, I met Chris at Wheelers nightclub in Leyton Road , Stratford E15, as you can tell Chris has been through the wars physically and mentally, and is on a even keel, years ago me, Chris and Rob, carried out our no nonsense vicious attacks on the heroin dealers and scum around the East End, about the time when I worked in the Queen Vic pub in Forest Gate doing the music. Chris is a funny, quick witted man with old school morals and respect. He says confidently he would die for me, and I know this to be true as he nearly did, and vice versa. We made some good money, but as before can't go into massive detail , just another violent and dark part of my life, Chris still lives in this dark world, that life is no longer for me, but if any one hurts me or my own, then I can soon turn into that dark world again, Chris has a good book in him, Chris is one of them unknown names, but is far more dangerous than most.

Billy Yates

Billy and Neil Charles

Neil Charles, he's now banged up, we were involved in all the drug dealer robberies. Neil is a real old school friend of me and Rob Josephs, a funny guy and a heart of gold. We saw some great action together, once Neil shot himself trying to un-jam a 9mm handgun lol he told the hospital it was a drive by ha ha ha Neil is still in the world I was.

Billy Yates

With this team of villains behind him, it was no way that Billy Yates was going to stay out of the radar of the police for long. It's one thing to have a name floating about amongst the whispers on the street; it's another thing when they eventually get a face to match up to it. Staying low key was easy when you was putting a loaded gun in the face of a drug dealer, taking their money and then binning their drugs, after all they aren't exactly going to go running to make a complaint to the police but they do go run to someone higher up the criminal food chain, who is now out of pocket in both money and their supplies. It wasn't long before the word was out to have these modern day Robin Hoods found and sorted which in turn also meant that it wasn't long before people who were out to make a name for themselves were trying their luck to take Billy and his friends out of the game. The problem then becomes that people with a vicious mentality like Billy weren't going to just sit back and take it, if you failed to do what you set out to do then beware because these guys would come for you.

I remember this one guy I was chasing down, parked up his car and ran into his house. I kept driving and put my car through the fella's house. When I got out of the car I was standing in the living room with the fella on the floor, gobsmack, shitting himself. Good old Volvo lol

Billy Yates

With this kind of retaliation and other criminal activates ranging from robbing a casino hustler for £45,000 to selling motorbikes that were then stolen back later in the night it wasn't long before police intelligence got to know what Billy looked like and were on the lookout for him.

Whilst making his way home from a girlfriend's house in Chingford, Billy got his first introduction to DC Hill and more importantly, DC Hill got his first introduction to Billy Yates. They say you can only make one first impression and this encounter stayed in both their minds for many years that followed.

Billy in cuffs

I was arrested by DC Hill and his buddies from Barkingside nick, they picked me up off the street and cuffed me while I was in Chingford. I was on the back seat of their car; they were chatting shit about what they think I'd been up to not really paying attention to me. I was a small built guy back then and I managed to get one of my hands out my cuffs and while the car was moving I reached for the door, rolled out and was up and running off into the distance over fences, fish ponds, etc away from the helicopter, through the back alleys until I was home free.

I still have the cuffs with DC Hill's name on them, I later rang DC Hill to tell him what a sloppy penis he was,

78

told him he was crap at his job, asked him how he felt, and were his pals laughing at him. After that he chased me for years... lol

Billy Yates

Being visible on the street wasn't a wise move after that close encounter so a new ploy to earn some money came about that allowed Billy to stay out of view. This involved advertising goods in the local paper or the Loot and having the potential buyers coming to a vacant address that the lads had got it to and when they buyers turned up, they would be informed the goods didn't exist and were then relieved of their money. What better way to rob people without searching for them in the open, just have them come to you and rob them out of view within a house. There was one occasion that this set up almost backed fired when a set of top of the range speakers were being 'sold' and the buyers turned up to 'buy' them. The problem with this transaction was the 'buyers' were out to rob the 'sellers' while the 'sellers' were out to rob the 'buyers'. Needless to say the situation reached a very sticky moment before common sense prevailed over instinct and the funny side was seen by both sides.

As with any scam involving the public, it wasn't long before the police were setting up their own sting by responding to one of their ads to catch the lads red handed. The day came when the undercover policeman turned up to buy his advertised goods, waiting for the deal to go down and then call in the back up. The only problem was one of the team were outside, saw the van of police that were in waiting and phoned the others who were in the house. Billy was upstairs when the shit it the fan for them.

Police came for me again in a sting operation in Manor Park, involving DC McCabe, dodgy fucker, but I got away again, this time from an upstairs rear window, over back gardens of a terraced street, being pursued by 4 big lumps (coppers) me jumping fences like a cat, them behind crashing and breaking everything as they followed. I kicked in some poor woman's back door to get away as the street was terraced, ran through the house jumped straight through the sash window, cutting myself badly (net curtains still around me – I still have the scars) hid in a wheelie bin for 45 minutes, bleeding and retching from the smell, as the police ran past the bin. I could hear them discussing and arguing, about where I had gone.

Billy Yates

Billy's luck of escaping the police was being tested to its limits when a year later he was finally arrested.

In 1994 I was renting a flat, 878 Romford Road, Manor Park E12, I had been using a fresh ID for about a year when I was raided, the police were told by my ex birds dad that I had stolen gear in my flat, I was 21 at the time. They found a few bits of catalogue stuff, 3 jumpers I think, unopened and in another name, so I was arrested for obtaining goods by deception. Freemans was free in them day's lol

So this crack team of CID officers took me to Forest Gate police station and whilst waiting for my duty solicitor I was allowed 1 phone call. So I rang Rumbalows to let them know I wouldn't be there that morning to receive the new telly and video I was waiting for, and gave them another date to deliver it. The copper next to me and the desk sergeant were laughing and said you got some front, lol I was bailed to return and never did, they kept the 3 jumpers and I got my TV and video.

About 3 months later I was in the Golden Fleece pub in Manor Park talking with Mickey Gluxstead (notorious East End villain) when one of the CID who nicked me came in at lunch time and ordered a drink at the bar he saw me sitting there with Mickey and gazed over at me. I could see the cogs turning in his brain trying to work out where he knew me from, lol he just stood there confused holding his pint, then Mickey clocked him and said to me 'what's this cunt looking at?' at which time the fella looked away, lol, Mickey had just got out of nick then.

Billy Yates

CHAPTER 6

It was at this point in his life that Billy found happiness with the love of his life, Tina Joseph. Tina was the cousin of Kelly McGivney, a woman Billy had been seeing on and off for the last 2 years.

Kelly did me nut in and I was friends with Tina whilst she was pregnant with Reece. Kelly cheated on me a couple of times so I left her and her and Tina had a fight over me in the exchange shopping centre in Ilford.

Like two mad cats lol and Kelly pulled out a bar on Tina. I walked away with Tina and have never looked back.

Billy Yates

Tina relaxing in Miami

I have been with Tina for nearly 15 years now, she has put up with so much shit from me it's unreal, not cheating or violence towards her but to other people, she has seen me with road rage and jumping out of cars at people I can't let things go sometimes. I love her more than she realises, and she still looks as sexy as ever, she was 17 when I met her and I was 21, I got fatter lol and she ain't fucking changed a bit.

She was pulled from pillar to post years ago, having to move every 5 minutes, to Spain, Miami, place to place, and living out of hotels all around the UK. We must have over 15 addresses over the years, where I live now is the longest I have lived in any one place and it's good to know the police ain't knocking anymore. I do have CCTV but that is just me. I will always be the same I suppose; Tina is a great mum and puts so much effort into our kids, Tina is my half Anglo Indian and half English queen.

Billy Yates

We met when Billy was with my cousin and my first serious boyfriend was in prison. Billy split up with her and a few times and it was on and off between them, I guess we just fell in love. when I first saw Billy I thought he was a bit of a asshole but then he grew on me, we had a tried and tested relationship, with him up and down from my loft from what seemed like constant police visits and the road rage where he nearly killed me and Kelly and the two fella's in the car with us at the time. My parents didn't like Billy as they were set on me staying with my ex, who was constantly in and out of prison for creepers (scum).

Billy was always at the window and over the back fence, dodgy passports, everything was dodgy about him back then, a few times the police visits were so constant he had to disappear for months at a time. It was his own fault as when he would escape from them, Billy being Billy, would wind them up, ringing them and calling them names and tormenting them, so he made it personal.

He's a good father and loves his kids; he's too soft with them and never has to give them a smack. We are both like friends with our kids and can talk to them about anything.

He was and still is like a kid at times, he used to do crazy things at the drop of a hat. I was embarrassed many a time; he even managed to get us a twelve month ban from every Tesco's store in the country, for starting on a security guard. He's my man and I love him and I hate him just as much most of the time.

Tina Joseph

With each new address Billy had to obtain to avoid being caught, he had to rely on having people around him that knew the score, people like his mates Mick and Martin from Limes Green Estate.

Michael, Mick, Billy and Martin

Mick lived in the flat directly below me on Limes Farm estate, Mick hid and helped me a couple of times when police raided my place and I returned the favour when police chased Mick through the car park. As Mick leaped over cars the police had no chance of catching him, I ran down after seeing what had happened and found Mick hidden in some hedges, after about 20mins of staying out of view he jumped in my car, laid on the back seat and I drove him to Hackney.

More recently, his dog fathered pups with mine, lol, he's a great fella with a wild and interesting past, he and his wife Ann are old school east end people.

Martin, another good friend of mine, he's a great fella and a good car painter.

Billy Yates

Billy always having to leave Tina when things got too hot for him really took its toll when Tina gave birth to her son, Reece.

Billy with Reece - 1997

Reece was born on the 29/5/95 to Tina's ex, a dirty crack head burglar and in Reece's life has been out for just 2 years, just a scumbag who steals from people's houses. Reece is a good kid he's my son and I'm his dad I want the best for him like I do all my kids.

Billy Yates

As Billy was settling in to his new home life he was also settling in to being a known name and face on the street with a fearful reputation. He was openly approached with illegal business ventures and Billy got involved with anything he knew would turn a pound note. One person in particular that was making a mint in ID fraud was an East End lad by the name of Paul Gordon.

I met Paul Gordon in 1995; he owned the mobile phone shop opposite the Thatched House pub in

Leytonstone High Road. I frequented the shop a lot, as those were the days when forging paperwork and utility bills were easy to obtain phone contracts, and Paul didn't care as he received, I think, something like £250 per contract he set up and you got a free brick phone in with the deal and these were the days before SMS messaging.

Paul was a clever black guy who was into his taking money for free scams including credit card cloning on a mobile PDQ machine; he had a flashy Toyota supra 3.0 turbo which I used to use and he liked a big ass girl with a pretty face working behind the counter.

I would take cards here and there off him and run plastic about and move massive amounts of benefit books about for him as he had a few great deals set up with the Nigerians , we were earning what I thought at the time was good money. We did a few mail order scams, and we would acquire dud credit cards from here and there and re programs them with fresh information.

I collected a couple of cards one day from Paul and used them, until one came on top for me and I was chased from a major supermarket caught and went into police custody for 5 days. whilst I was shipped around to 3 different police stations, then I was up in Bow magistrates court and thought 'fuck me what a result' when I got bailed. Then when I went back down to the court cells to be released I was re arrested by Dagenham CID over other various charges and stayed there for a couple of days before appearing at Barking magistrates court where I was found guilty of criminal damages when I escaped from police a couple of years previous by jumping through the old ladies window. the CPS told the court that Mr. Martindale kicked the back door off a terraced house whilst running from pursuing officers and did not hesitate and jumped straight through the front room sash window, SAS style (CPS words not mine) and took off with the net curtains still round him and police subsequently didn't apprehend him on that occasion.

It was quite hard to keep a straight face as they read this out to the judge and whilst in the dock I looked down to see a grinning Gary Jacobs, the famous radio and TV solicitor. This time I didn't get bail, I was so happy to be on my way to prison as I fucking hate those police cells... You get so fed up of reading the same graffiti over and over again.

Billy Yates

It was on February the 27th 1996 when the steel door closed behind Billy and without the opportunity to make a run for it, it was only a matter of time before the past of Manea will come to surface and haunt him.

Being inside was not as bad as I thought, food was shite, people were cool and I made some good friends. I was on B wing at first as when they sent me down on remand I was on record as a police absconder, so I had 23 hour bang up and had to wear a half green and half yellow suit for a month and had to have a screw with me every time I left the cell.

I was banged up with a fella called Scotch Andy, who had ran a sword through some fella in a pub in Manor Park, and a murderer who shot two black fella's in Dalston during a bout of road rage and Billy 'Jango 'Williams.

I was also banged up with Patrick Gallagher an Irish traveller and a good boxer, he was at one point gonna go pro with Frank Warren, his nickname was 'blue boy'; he messed up his career through his various crimes, a real nice fell.

Billy Yates

Inside Pentonville Prison

Although Billy adjusted fast to his incarceration his own personal demons of needing acceptance were surfacing, and whilst amongst the general population, Billy found solace with the Islamic section of the prison and it wasn't long before he turned to Islam and became a devout Muslim.

I was stuck in a cell for 23 hours a day. I said I was interested in learning about Islam because it meant I could spend more time out of the cell but I actually got quite into it.

I turned to Islam and took my shahadda inside, got in with the Muslim brothers, as they took me in without question. I can fully understand why so many people do believe in the teaching of Islam as the bound within the community is strong and loyal.

Billy Yates

Even though he had adopted the peaceful notion of not to make the first strike, it wasn't long before Billy had to be his old self in a display of prison survival 101.

I was moved to G wing where I was allowed more freedom and we had a telly and pool table. then I had a row with a black fella who said he was gonna wet me up , so I done him with a tin of tuna and he took his belt off, but I got too many blows in with the tuna, we were dragged away and I was sent back to B wing and 23hrs of closed doors.

Then after many applications for bail and on August 8th I got 'Judge and Chambers' bail and visited Ray in Maidstone nick, then didn't return to court. I was back on the run.

After my release I would go to Finsbury Park mosque and I once had dinner with Abu Hamza. I had no trouble with him and he didn't fill me with hate.

Billy Yates

Billy had used his outside contacts and got hold of a new passport and other various bits of ID, got Tina to leave

Reece with her mother and to meet him. They boarded the first flight to Miami.

Miami was soooo hot, people were friendly, great night life in South beach but all about the $$$$$$$$$$$$$$$$$$$$$$$$$$$$$$

Billy Yates

Miami pool, South beach

Once back in the UK, Billy used the contacts given to him by his new Muslim brothers to stay below the police radar.

Once on the outside I went deep deep into Islam, I hung around with Abu Hamza (the hook) and Sheik Fazal, both now locked up.... I got Tina to convert to Islam; we got our union blessed in a Masjid in Manor Park. I was white; I could go places and get things done for these people, if you get my drift. I left Islam when things started to get heavy.

I can't say too much about this for legal reasons, which have come about recently.

I have massive respect for people who follow that faith but I found it too restrictive and just couldn't do it.

Billy Yates

Billy used his new found faith to help guide him to walk a path straight and true. He even took up a day job to earn honest money but after a short while temptation struck and Billy found himself back to his old ways, stealing money to survive.

Once he knew where the money was hidden before the tally up at day's end, he had it away and was soon signing up for all sorts of retail jobs where he could do the same again. Something that his pal, Chris Stafford can testify to.

What can I say about Billy that not already been said!!! to this day I'm not 100% sure how bill came into my life, I think through a friend of a friend, my first recollection of Bill was a cold winters night down Southend sea front, when this guy (I now know to be Bill) raced up on an 1000cc r1 motorcycle and started burning up the rear tyre and filled the whole street with rubber smoke in front of 4/5 old bill cars then whilst still spinning the wheel raced off down the front... childish I know but I thought mate this guy is off his nut.

We got talking and our friendship grew from there, that was about 12 years ago, Billy used to get into all sorts of things, I remember this one time Billy turned up at my flat in Benfleet with a bag full of cash and a copy of the loot newspaper, he told me he had just taken it from a place where he was working because he thought he deserved it as a bonus.

He always makes you laugh lol Billy and I spent many nights kicking round different car events and street races, cars seemed to be our lives back then. I have hundreds of stories to tell about Bill, including the 4 am prank calls to classified ads, lol Billy was doing it long before Steve Penk.

What with the scams, debt collecting, door work, the list goes on and on, but one thing is for sure though if Billy trusts you, you have a real friend for life, he will help you out no matter what but be warned though if you cross him or knock him or upset him, there will be a price to pay.

Billy does not bully his friends or the average bloke in the street, or run round beating people for no reason, he once said to me no one gets done who don't deserve it!! and how true that is, he is the king of karma he's not the one that goes around, he's the one that comes around...lol even my parents love Bill to pieces and he's such a giggle to have around, always makes us laugh at the things he's been up to, we wish him all the best - there is only one Billy.

Chris Stafford

Chris Stafford and Billy

Being back in to the violence game meant Billy had to get back into shape from living the easy life and was soon getting into the gym on a regular basis.

I started training at Wag Bennets in Forest Gate, an old converted church in Romford Rd, Arnold Schwarzenegger trained there in the 70's. I then trained at Fort Galaxy gym in Ilford, Connaught Lane, owned by a huge man called Dean McTurnan, a nice bloke, I like Dean.

Billy Yates

Billy after training for 8 months, natural no shit or steroids - 1997

With any progression in violence and weight training, Billy was offered work as a doorman and it was in this profession that Billy met the man who would become his best friend and partner in crime, Paul Meeking.

A rare friend, 1 in a million, he's always there for me. I can say all my family and friends love Paul.

Billy Yates

(xxxl)Paul Meeking and Billy

I first met Bill about twelve years ago when I was working on the door I was asked to do a night at some club and Bill was the head doorman after a couple of months I was asked to do somewhere else and lost contact with him. we met quite by accident about a year later in a fishing tackle shop in Barkingside and renewed our friendship, after a couple of months we parted company again. Then we met up again when he came into a pub I was working and took up our friendship up again. This was the pattern that followed for the next eight years which I found out later on was on the run. The last two years I've got to know Bill very well to the point of having Sunday dinner with his family quite regularly. His two boys think the world of me, his daughter lily calls me granddad, my son and his two sons go ice skating most Saturdays.

Right now about Bill, me and Bill have had our moments together from stand up full blown rows and then something silly. For example we was in a pub in Brentwood and Bill got me a vodka and red bull which I declined because I don't like vodka this upset Bill and we had a big row shouting and screaming at each other, all the people in the pub went round to the other bar and left us to it, after ten minutes we walked back round to the other bar as if nothing had happened finding out no one not even the governor wanted to come round and get between us.

me, Billy and Roy Shaw went to Sam's one night and they wouldn't let us in, so Roy talks to the manager while the doorman run out to me and Billy who turns round to one of them and says 'what do you want slimfast?' some Spaniard ran out and Bill said 'what do you want Bosnian Bob?' then said the manager looked like Alan Carr. later on the Spanish bloke came over and said 'I came out to help the doorman and saw you two and thought fuck that and went back in' he also bought us a bottle of pink champagne.

one day we were in Tesco's garage and I had an armful of beers and wine when bill came up behind me a pulled my tracksuit bottoms and pants down in front of two cashiers and about five customers. He also did that again when I was putting up his Xmas lights, I was up a ladder when he lent out of the window and pulled them down again. In the last year Bill has turned his life around, I've helped put a roof on a church where someone tried to nick the tiles, built a shed in his back garden and landscaped his garden. I've also done other things for him but cannot put them to print. All through the rows, the phone calls late at night to do job, I've always stood by him and always will. To sum Billy up a great friend to have but a bad man to cross also he doesn't suffer fools or plastic wannabe's.

Paul Meeking

With regular money coming in, all cash in hand, Billy thought it was time to get a place that he, Tina and young Reece could call home.

27 Fiennes Close, Dagenham. We moved in the week Princess Diana died.

L to R – Lew Yates, Billy, Big Joe Egan and Roy Shaw

The name of the petrol station says it all

Joy, she was like a mother to me and I a son to her

Cooking with Billy

After years on the run, former gangster has turned his life around

Ex-fugitive is walking tall to boost charity

Rhiannon Evans
rhiannon.evans@gazettenews.co.uk

Photo: Andy Palmer

AFTER years of giving police the runaround, a self-confessed ex-gangster is hoping to encourage others to take a walk for charity.

Ongar-based William Martindale says he spent more than 14 years on the run from the authorities facing a whole host of charges, including armed robbery.

But now the father-of-three is turning his life around and dedicating his time to fundraising for Great Ormond Street after being inspired by the help staff at the London hospital gave the son of a close friend, who has Downs syndrome.

"He got a great deal from the hospital - they are doing good things for people all the time," he said.

IN TRAINING: Fundraiser William is in training for his sponsored walk to raise cash for Great Ormond Street Hospital. He also plans top visit schools to tell youngsters about the importance of steering clear of crime.

> "I spent a lot of taxpayers' money making the boys in blue chase me ... now I want to put something back"

So, starting with a sponsored walk and with a wide variety of future events such as celebrity auctions, the 34-year-old is hoping to give the children's hospital a real boost.

"I spent a lot of the taxpayers' money making the boys in blue chase me, so I just want to put something back," he said.

"I'll also feel better about myself - I'm not a bad person. I'm just misunderstood and a bit of a rogue so I got sucked in with a crowd and ended up doing what I had to do. I didn't hurt anyone.

"For me though, it's turned out well - it could have gone a lot worse."

He spent several short spells in jail in his time, as a result of his work as a "doorman, debt collector, enforcer and problem solver".

Now, settled in Cripsey Avenue for more than three years with his family, William is working on his autobiography - which has the working title Running with the Devil. My 14 Years Avoiding the Long Arm of the Law - the proceeds of which will be donated to charity.

"People change and different things happen to you.

"I don't hold a grudge against the police they were just doing their job and I was just doing mine.

"It's so nice to be settled down now. Imagine 14 years on the run - it wears you down.

"I was constantly at the window every time I heard a noise.

"It's quite an experience, but it's not one I would recommend.

"Now I'm looking forward to going around schools and turning youngsters away from doing what I did."

Giving back to the community

103

Battle scars – nuff said – Chris Donnolly

Me and Rob - 2007

Me with my Buddy from my days in Manea, Jimmy Beanie

Freddy Shepherd and Paul Meeking

Billy with Tommy Fitzgerald and Rob Josephs

Roy Shaw and my Dad, Lew Yates – squaring off

CHAPTER 7

It was in 1997 when Lew phoned Billy to tell him that his best friend, Tommy Shepherd was in the paper, he had been found down a lane near the 16 foot river bank, he had been murdered. As soon as Billy read the paper that Lew had gotten to him, he felt choked up and gutted. He had no idea where's Tommy's parents were to talk to them, it had been years since he last saw them although he last saw Tommy a year previous. It was at that meeting that Tommy told Billy how he got married after Billy left Manea and had fathered 5 children, but his first child died after 3 weeks of cot death.

Tommy's death left me numb, people died from that incident, leave it at.

Billy Yates

Mr and Mrs Shepherd were told of the news of that a body that resembled their son was found on the 13th of April after a young lad who was out riding his bike, stopped to take a leak and discovered Tommy's legs sticking out of a pile of wood that was being used to hide his body at Horseway Drove. Mr Shepherd went down the crime scene where he was told to stand back; it was at that point that he knew that the body was defiantly his son's, who had been away from home for the past week. A few hours later, after matching his fingerprints, it was confirmed to them that it was in fact Tommy's body.

It took a month before the police called in their two main suspects, Neil Briggs and Jason Venie, two known Heroin users. They confessed to dumping his naked body there on the Tuesday before, rolled up in a carpet. Previously they had all been in the flat that Neil Briggs and Joanne Hall shared, along with Sarah Smith when a fella known as Tubby knocked on the door to sell them some 'stuff'. Tommy wanted nothing to do it the goods on offer so took himself into the other room and fell asleep on the settee. The next morning they apparently discovered Tommy dead, so they bathed him, wrapped him up and put him in the back of a truck to take him to the dump site, which was a gathering point for drug users. Forensics discovered that Tommy was actually still alive and slowly suffered for two days whilst bundled under a pile of wood. The excuse that Tommy was a drug user was given and that he died of an overdose, yet close friends, when interviewed, said that he never took drugs. Another point was raised to the use of his car; it was asked if he was going to go that far away to use drugs, why didn't he drive himself there or at least remove his vehicle off the double yellow lines he was parked on. Also it was found that Tommy had received a total of £4,500 after selling one of his horses, in cash, yet the money was not to be found.

When asked about the money they said they burnt the money along with his clothes and had wrapped Tommy's body up in a futon style mattress. They also said they burnt all the furniture and carpet that was in their flat, in fact when the police went round to arrest Neil at that address they found the place had been completely refurnished with brand new stuff. All four people known to have been at the scene were questioned, Neil and Jason, plus their partners, Joanne Hall and Sarah Smith and kept on remand. Sarah made a statement that she wasn't at the flat at the time; Jason had collected her and took her there. Upon seeing Tommy's body, she insisted that they report it to the authorities, Jason told her no. Then, when she needed to return home to pick up something, Jason went with her to ensure that she did not phone the police or ambulance crew, even though Tommy was still alive and there could have been a chance of saving him.

It was also summarised that amongst the other people involved were two drug dealers, Tommy and George Scott, but nothing could be proven.

Another name that was banded about was a man called, Dave Lenahan, who told police that Tommy's had driven him to Neil Brigg's flat and in the car was drug parafanilla including needles and syringes. It came to light that Neil and Jason moved Tommy's car from its spot outside the flat to a lay-by heading towards Peterborough, after they were spotted by a passerby. When the car was found, there was no drug parafanilla found.

Neil and Jason were charged with murder and by the time it went to Crown Court it had been reduced to manslaughter. It was during the hearing that a biased character witness, PC Betts from March police station, said that in his opinion, Tommy Shepherd was the kind of person who would of have used drugs. It was based on this testimony that the case was eventually dismissed without any charges of murder or manslaughter being made; instead they got 2 years for concealment. Even though at the inquest, which only Neil Briggs attended out of the accused, the toxologist's report showed that there were not enough drugs in Tommy's system to warrant a death by overdose plus there were no markings to indicate regular drug use. It was proven that the heroin found in his blood stream originated from his mouth, most likely put in a drink and digested orally.

Just another example of a flawed criminal justice system that could not see what anyone else looking at the case could, and that is simply a man was killed by drug users for the money he was carrying on him. Whoever heard of druggie's burning £4500 and yet still having enough savings to buy all new furniture? Why clean the body before dumping it? Why not call the police or ambulance? Why conceal the body amongst other items and dispose of it down by a river bank? Too many questions can be raised by the events admitted to by those arrested.

It was after the hearing that PC Betts arrived at the home of the Shepherd's with threats of ripping their home apart in search for the body of Dave Lenahan, who had gone missing. It was believed that Dave was buried on their property, Mrs. Shepherd made it quite clear to the officer that he's body wouldn't be found here, because if they had got hold of him and killed him, his body would have been put up on the side of the road with a big sign on him stating for all to see that they 'GOT ONE OF THEM!'

The Shepherd family has made it quite clear that even to this day, if those involved are ever found, they will be made to pay.

People wanted revenge and a lot of people went missing at that time.

I know that Tommy was murdered by junkies. They just wanted to steal £4,500 from him to get drugs and they poisoned him.

These scumbags will be looking over their shoulders for the rest of their lives, People are out their looking for them and I'd love to run into them myself.

Billy Yates

Billy at the grave site of his departed friend, Tommy Shepherd

CHAPTER 8

After the shocking news that his friend had been killed, Billy became enraged and targeted drug dealers of all levels to seek vengeance.

In the early days I would rob businesses and post offices, I'd never target individual people or mug old ladies. But after Tommy's death all I'd do, is do over drug dealers.

I hate drugs - I've seen them destroy so many people's lives.

Billy Yates

There was no stopping his rampage as his temper was controlled by a short fuse.

I was embarrassed the most of all one day when Bill gave me and my neighbour a lift somewhere and we stopped in a bit of traffic on Green Lanes in Dagenham. We were stuffed full in the car, with our two children and my neighbours. As we were sitting in traffic, Billy had his window open and was on his mobile, some fella, about 23, was walking past us and whilst Bill was on the phone, Bill looked at this fella who was looking at us and the fella said "what" with right attitude. To this Billy said to his mate on the phone 'hold on, I will ring you back', he jumped straight out of the car and walked up to the cocky fella, the fella dropped his rucksack he was carrying and that was it, Billy just hit him once and he went on all fours and seemed to fall straight down like someone took his legs from him, the fella was on all fours wobbling like an animal that had just been darted with a tranquilizer. Billy shouted 'see what you get for being cocky, you mug' and jumped back in the car, and we drove off. I was so embarrassed.

Another time Billy had old shitty beige Ford Fiesta, and we were at the traffic lights in Hainault, it was a light Friday evening and this car full of lads about our age pulled up next to us at the lights. They looked like they were in their mummy's shiny rover, brand new, and were laughing and sneering at us in Bills old fiesta. Billy didn't worry about how many fella's were in the car, he opened his window and they exchanged swear words, at which point the lights changed and people were honking their horns, so we pulled away and they slowed to let Bill catch up. Bill slammed his car into the side of theirs, "crash" he managed to do this twice, before their faster car got away, mad I know but I will never forget the colour run from their faces and the change in their expressions, as if to say omg this bloke is not well, and believe me he wasn't at times , he's temper can be terrible, he can't let things go and if someone upsets him in the slightest he's of like a bomb and cannot let it just rest.

Tina Joseph

Billy was given a reason to be happy and forget about his violent behaviour when his son Lewis was born into this world.

Lewis was born on the 4/5/98 he's just like me, a little wind up and loves anything to do with nature. He can't have enough pets, it's like a zoo here and he wants to do what I did and work as a zoo keeper or the RSPCA or something similar. He's 10 now and is a very bright kid, so I'm going to push him in the right direction, I'm proud of all my kids and we throw ourselves into Halloween and Christmas as much as possible.

Billy Yates

Billy with Lewis - 2000

23 days later, a legend in the bare knuckle and unlicensed fight game lost his bout with cancer, he's name was Lenny Mclean.

A wreath displaying the fighting title of Lenny McLean –
The Guv'nor

Lenny was the type of man usually referred to by polite society as a "colourful character". Cockney blood coursed through every vein of his 6ft 3in, 20-stone body. He was a bare-knuckle prize-fighter, a nightclub bouncer, a convicted criminal and, most recently, an actor and author.

Among the mourners was the obligatory scattering of sharp-suited men in dark glasses. Some of them were not just playing the part. Tony Lambrianou, for instance, who served 15 years for his part in the murder of Jack "the Hat" McVitie and standing by his side was Charlie Kray, older brother of the twins.

Also in attendance was Lew Yates, who had put a challenge out to Lenny back in their fighting days. A challenge that was never answered but respect was given by all on this sombre day. Billy was with Lew on that day and was introduced to a number of known villains and criminals that knew his father. One in particular was Danny Woollard, a well respected face from the East End that was a major player alongside Mickey Gluxstead and the Hunt firm.

I have only known bill for a few years since I met him at Lenny's funeral, I personally have known Billy's dad for years, and I can say they are from the same mould.

Lew was an awesome fighter and has a massive reputation, I know of Billy through our East End circles, he's a great kid and a go getter, no nonsense, no bullshit and a down to earth nice fell.,

Good luck with the book Billy boy.

Danny Woollard

Danny Woollard jnr, Danny Woollard, Roy Shaw and Billy

I like Danny, he knows everyone, he's a likable bloke and he ring's me often for a chat. A dangerous man and ex robber. Well respected.

I first met Danny at Lenny McLean's funeral just before he got another big bit of bird for guns and body bags lol

Billy Yates

Billy's notoriety over the coming years after mixing with people like Danny Woollard soon grew and it wasn't long before he was classed as one of their own big well known and respected legends in the gangland circles, two of which were fighting celebrity Roy Shaw and known villain Billy Blundell.

My friendship with Roy started back in 2000 when I met him in the Epping Forest Country Club, I walked over to him and introduced myself as my dad fought him in 1981, he realised who I was and bought me a drink. Being polite I took it even though I didn't drink, every time he turned his back I just tipped it into a nearby plant, and pretended I had drank it. He then invited me to his house and we had some pictures done, I went out with him and my pal mark the next week. we met in the Royal Oak in Loughton , where Roy did his party trick and stuck a cigarette in the end of his cock and said look I've started smoking again, and then chewed up a glass, from which he had drank from lol

We did have a fall out over something, as Roy can't have people to close to him for too long as he turns on them, he has a lot of love and can be very generous, and then he can be a real old bastard. He does not have many people round him for long, he calls you all the cunts then forgets he's said it and rings up like nothing has happened and apologises when you tell him.

So I left him alone for a few years whilst being on the run and popped in to say hello once in a while. I was at Roy's house when the planes hit in Sep 11th 2001.

As of late Roy has not been himself, so I have grown a lot closer to Roy after he was ripped off for a few hundred grand. I have had a few good nights out with Roy to the Sugar Hut in Brentwood, the Edge run by 'bad breath' John in Epping and the 195 in Epping, amongst other places.

Billy Yates

Roy Shaw and Billy

My name is Roy Shaw... Billy is my pal, he has a great personality, you can take him anywhere and he creates an atmosphere wherever he goes. He just has a huge amount of confidence and he makes the night whenever we go out, he also is a great knowledge of most things and knows so many people, he never fails to surprise me. He has helped me in many ways, with my business, computers, websites and day to day things like my car, TV, garden etc I have told Bill he's up there with Joe Pyle, a true friend.

I know some people don't like Bill, as he's straight talking and does not give a fuck who he upsets or gets in his way, our friendship has been tested recently as certain people have been jealous, what these people don't realize is that me and Billy's dad Lew 'wild thing' Yates, have been pals for over 30 years.... so my advice to you is do not upset bill as he will never back down to anybody.

he has a wicked streak which runs through him if you cross him which I have seen myself when we was on a night out in Brentwood, Essex, and the door staff locked themselves in the club called Sam's. Billy wanted to bite their noses off ha ha ha that's one of bills sayings "I will bite ya nose off ya cunt " Billy has a kind side which not to many people see, he would help an old lady across the road. Billy is keeping his nose clean nowadays and is back in training so beware. I wish him all the luck in the world, and thanks for all you have done for me mate good luck with the book.

Roy 'pretty boy' Shaw

John 'Gaffer' Rollinson and Billy Blundell

Billy Blundell and I first met in 2000; Billy and my dad have always had respect for each other from way back. When I met Billy and told him who I was he was over the moon and took me straight in. He made me so welcome it's untrue; I stayed over at his house and trained at his gym, had dinner with him and spent a few good times with him. Billy is a clever clever man a real 1000% diamond with old school respect and a great family. I just hated his bastard

120

dog that he had on a chain outside his bungalow, the fucking thing went for everyone, and they say dog like owner and all that. Even though my dad had a fall out with Billy and his minders years ago, Bill moves forward and that's the past attitude, I can't speak highly enough of Billy Blundell.

I took my dad round to Bills in 2000 and we had dinner in his luxury bungalow in Bulphan on the A128, all stone floors, and massive layout. Billy is one clever and respected man, was always 1 step ahead of the old bill, never had to do masses of time, as he was clever enough not to get caught, and knew who to trust, gaffer was his minder for a few years. Gaffer is a nice fella, I just got off the phone with him today and I must say look out for gaffer's new book as it's gonna be blinding.

Billy Blundell even lent me his bright red Rolls Royce on my 28th birthday so I could go out for a meal with Tina and he even filled it up with petrol for me. I cannot speak highly enough of Billy, a real old school gent who always gives you the old style mafia kiss on the cheek and a hug when he sees you off. Billy's mum is now 95 and he has always looked after his old mum, a real family man, family comes first to Billy and that shines through.... Good luck Billy and a healthy life to you mate.

P.S. that bottle of brandy I owe you is on its way, luv ya

Billy Yates

Billy was still working as a bouncer, amongst other things, to earn extra money for his growing family. By now he had worked venues in London, Essex and Kent.

My first door was with Mickey Bennett at the Army and Navy pub in Chelmsford, for Raven Security run by the

121

UK chapter of Hell's Angels. Then the Litten Tree in Old Street, followed by Legends in Sittingbourne, Kent, the Connaught Rooms, and the Cauliflower with XXXL Paul (Meeking), the Castle in Plaistow and T.J's in Silver Town.

I worked in some really dodgy bars in east London and there was always trouble. I have been stabbed on three separate occasions whilst working the doors.

Billy Yates

Two of those stabbings happened in just mere weeks of each other. Billy was stabbed in the back in 2001 at the castle pub in Plaistow with an ice pick and that was followed two weeks later with someone stabbing him in his right arm where the tip of the knife broke off as it embedded into his bone, on top of that he was then gassed in his face and ear.

I like my blood, you either panic or go mental, and I'm the latter.

Billy Yates

It was around this time that Billy first met Ian Radford.

I met Bill in 2001 through a mutual contact when I was looking for a labourer, they gave me Bill's number, after a conversation with him and meeting him for the first time he seemed to be a nice chap.

How fucking wrong I was!! I suffered this man for one year!!

We worked on various jobs together, I found Bill to always be on time and hard working, we got on well together both having similar back grounds and a good sense of humour sometimes a bit twisted but hay it's all good fun !!

One time he brought his gimp friend to work called Anthony a bit of a simple country lad. I had Bill digging out footings for £65 a day but he had Anthony doing it for £10 a day so Bill is stood round watching his big mole dig. I wasn't happy, when the owner of the house asked who Anthony was Bill said 'its Ian's son'. The cheeky Bastard!! But we kept Anthony on for the day. Bill had him running around making animal noises and showing me how fast a fat lad could run. Bill kept him at it all day, I know you shouldn't laugh but it was so funny by the end of the day I was hurting from laughter,

I been friends with bill ever since, we have had many laughs.

I consider Bill a close friend and I would back him up 100% BUT never lend him money, you won't get the fucker back lol, just joking

Then I made the big mistake of inviting Bill to my salsa dancing night in Brentwood, never fucking again. He turned up with his mate xxxl Paul, all dressed in their big bomber jackets, half cut, Bill abused Paul (jokingly) as his big gay mate and was little loud so the salsa instructor stopped the class and asked Bill to keep the noise down, which Bill replied, 'ok, sorry fella', but fair play to Bill he was only having a laugh, and talking to a couple of my friends. About 20 minutes go by and with all the laughter and noise coming from the bar the salsa instructor fella got stroppy with bill and came across rude, so Bill has now lost it a little, as Bill thought he was doing nothing wrong. Bill says 'go on mate, fuck off and dance', to which the instructor pulled his Madonna mike off and shouted to the barman, 'out, out, throw him out; I don't want that man in here'. The barman looked at Bill and said, 'no way, you throw him out!' and then proceeded to give Bill free drinks all night. at the end of the night Bill went over to the instructor and put his arm round him and said 'how much did I pay to get in here?' the instructor said '£6.00' so Bill says 'give me the fucker back, as you didn't teach me a thing!' Bill got his money and we all left, never again.

Ian Radford

Ian, his wife Madeline and Billy

I met Ian in 2001, he's a builder and he asked me if I wanted some cash work, I agreed and I was his labourer for about a year. Then work went quiet and so I stopped working for him, whilst I was working for him we became best mates and had many laughs at work. He's had a very turbulent past and was raised in children's homes, up north in Yorkshire, he was born in Scotland, he's father was from Yugoslavia, so he got it from all angles. Ian is not the biggest of men but has the heart of a lion, as brave as fuck and also a kind man, he can sometimes be as tight as a ducks arse lol. I could never work for him again as he can't pay me enough lol and he says I'm too hard to control lol, but if there is ever any trouble he's there for me and vice versa.

He helped me repair the church roof and he's into his big bikes like me, I love him and his family. His other half Madeline is a lovely girl, and we all get on great, Ian has also has 3 great kids Charlie, Brook and Sonny.

Ian recently started salsa classes, lmao dirty old man we all know why he really goes lol he's become an expert at this weird dance lol and can swoop across the largest room like Lionel Blair, almost as if he's on roller skates ha ha ha.

Billy Yates

Working cash in hand jobs were essential for Billy has he couldn't have his name, national insurance number and such like details on file for him to be traced. It was at times like this where he had to constantly hide behind false identities that life on the run was proving tiring for a man who just wanted to get on and enjoy the basic things in life.

Being on the run was hard but a buzz, forever young or so I thought, some people dream of going to Miami and having nice cars, I dreamt of passing my test and having insurance. I got tired of having to pretend to pick my nose as if I wasn't bothered when the police looked at me in traffic. The police look at you and know the signs of no Licence or insurance lol it's all body language. Since passing my test in 2007 I try but just can't get a pull lol It's one of them things I dreamt of

when I was on the run, was getting pulled over and I could jump out of the car and say 'Fuck off, I'm legal' lol

Billy Yates

Another thing still missing in Billy's life was a connection with his mother, Jean. Being a parent himself now he thought it was still to find his estranged Mum and hoping get the peace he needed.

Billy hadn't seen his mother for 24 years when he made contact with her.

I didn't even know what she looked like. She was just a friendly elderly lady - a complete stranger - there will never be a bond or a proper relationship between us.

My Mum can't put back what's lost or turn the clock back but she's my Mum, what can I say? I love her but we both don't know how to love each other. My Mum from when I was 3 has gone and in a way is dead to me; all we have is what's left. It's no good being angry, anger eats you away, if I'm angry I will direct it at another person who I feel need it, to learn from being punished.

Billy Yates

CHAPTER 9

The winds of change were starting to blow for Billy, years of his antics and pissing off the wrong people were coming back to haunt him. One occasion in particular with a drug dealer led to Billy being shot at in Chigwell in 2002.

I'd received a phone call and been told to meet somebody at a garage to collect a debt, but I'd been set up. A drug dealer I'd done over wanted me dead and three people turned up in a car with a shotgun. I saw the barrel of the gun out of the car window and the bullet scraped my arm. I grabbed the gun and they sped off so I hurled it at the car.

Billy Yates

Billy standing by the garage door that still bears the damage from the shotgun blast

A few months later, Billy found himself getting involved in yet another crime that gave the police reason to want to find him.

A friend's girlfriend got raped. She went to police and somebody was arrested but the case was dropped because she couldn't face going to court.

I found him and made sure he would never do anything like that again.

Billy Yates

Billy escaped the police using one of his false passports, he travelled to Spain and the charges were dropped against him in his absence due to lack of evidence after the witness backed out.

Upon his return saw further problems for him arise after he went to collect some much needed finances.

Steve Brown and Will Bainbridge owed me some money, its 'alleged' I shot holes in their workshop door. They see me coming; they closed the doors, locking me out. It's also 'alleged' I then spoke to them cowering behind a car through the hole which the sawn off had made.

They both made statements to the police in 2003, wankers; I got even in the end. I found Steve and stripped him naked in Hainault Forest, I made him dig his grave and then I beat him. He suffered 5 broken ribs. After that they both went into hiding, no one as seen them since.

Billy Yates

It wasn't long after they made their statements that Billy's known address was raided by the police. Billy had to move, he stayed with his friend Steve, who had recently lost his brother Simon. Simon, took his own life after being involved with drugs, Billy was friends with both of them.

Simon's headstone

Simon was a good friend who lived in Chigwell, near where I used to have a place. Drugs again, he was coked up and pissed, had a row with his bird and hung himself from the stairs. After he died, I was raided for guns in 2003, so I was living there with his brother Steve until things died down. It was a bit weird walking up them stairs each day.

Billy Yates

Shortly after this, Billy laid low for a couple of years, earning what he could where he could until he had enough to move   Tina and the kids out of the areas they had always stayed in and out to a more rural setting like he was brought up in. In 1995 they got a house in Ongar, Essex and Billy went about his business undetected, his neighbours thinking he was just another London boy starting over. Acting like a local, Billy amerced himself into the day to day lives of those around him; one of them people was Jim Thorpe, landlord of the Blackhorse pub.

I've known Bill for about 3 years, the first time I met was on a Tuesday night, and I remember that because one of my barmaids was in having a drink. Bill and his brother were talking about motorbikes and Kim, my off duty barmaid, joined in on their conversation by saying she had a bike, to which Bill asked what sort she had, Kim's reply was a 50cc scooter. Billy nearly spat his drink all over her, laughing. My first impression of Bill was that he seemed rough and ready, not someone you expect to see that often in a country pub. Well that's where I was wrong, Bill came in a few more times, then we got talking and he said he was living in the next village. I got on well with him and after a few months it was like we had known each other for years.

He is a down to earth bloke who would do anything for any one, a few of the regulars in the pub did not take to him but what do you expect with village people that never set foot outside the village. I've nearly barred him a few times for upsetting a few of them but thinking about it now, in any pub in the East End, no one would take any notice.

Bill is a great bloke and has brought me some good trade on a few occasions, with his Dad's book signing and a few other things. I've only known him a few years but I class him as a good friend. All the best Bill.

Jim Thorpe

Billy, Roy Shaw and Jim Thorpe, Landlord of Bill's local, the
Black Horse

*Jim is a good friend and a cocky, funny fucker. I
like Jim a lot; it's a shame to see him leave the pub soon.*

Billy Yates

Billy also found a kindred spirit in an elderly woman
named Joy, who was fending for herself as her husband Keith
was in hospital as a long term patient. Over the following
year and a half they became very close friends. It was after
Keith was finally discharged and given a clean bill of health
that tragedy stroke and Joy passed away.

*Joy, the most loveliest woman I have ever known.
She could see right through me for who I was. I wish I had
more time with her; she was like a mother, the only mother
I ever knew. So kind with a heart of gold and always a huge
smile, I loved her.*

She told her husband Keith, 'I will never let that boy down'. She called me her rebellious son.

William Martindale

Joy by name, Joy by nature the loveliest woman Billy has ever known

I look after Keith now that his wife Joy as passed away. She was like a Mum to me, we were so close.

William Martindale

Keith and Billy

It was whilst living this easy and quiet life that Billy took his ever watchful eye off the ball and started to fall back into the persona of William Martindale, falsely believing that all was ok. His family was still growing as Tina was pregnant with their third child.

Billy with his princess, Lilly

My princess Lilly, she is very demanding as all two year olds are, she is the light of my life, and no matter how sad or pissed off I'm feeling she always makes me laugh.

You think you know love but until you have children you don't know love, she's my little dolly, and I will not be letting her out until she's 30 lol

William Martindale

Billy was starting up his own business which was an honest trade so it needed him to be honest on his paperwork. All those years of avoiding such things were undone in a matter of weeks and once his name and address were on the system, the police that had been searching for him knew where to find their man.

The news headline the next day

At 04:30am on August 4th 2006, 30 armed police surrounded my house, there was no way out, I had been caught

William Martindale

The search warrant for Billy's house

The main reason for the armed response team was the outstanding investigation into the firearm charge from 2003. Whilst in custody Billy was also questioned on two murders that he was suspected of being involved in, one took place in 1996, the victim was thrown from a 14 storey window and the other took place in 1998 where a man was shot in Forest Gate, the man in question reportedly owed Billy £10,000 at the time. Billy made the statement that he had no involvement in either case.

Upon searching his property, no firearms were found so no charge was made.

In 2006, when I was arrested, both Steve Brown and Will Bainbridge withdrew their statements because they didn't want to go to court and face me over the dock. No gun, no charge lol

Billy Yates

On top on that, the case files from Manea had been destroyed over time by poor weather conditions soaking through the police house storeroom roof.

Although wanted over the years for questioning on a number of charges, Billy's involvement was never actually proved and so those cases were never followed up.

The only other outstanding issue was his absconding whilst on Judge and Chambers bail, a bail that should never have been issued in the first place due to the amount of time Billy had already served in prison when the appeal went in. But it seemed the same clerical error that appeared to make it happen in the first place also seemed to bury it.

Billy walked out a free man with no outstanding warrants on his head.

CHAPTER 10

With no warrants in his name, what would any normal person do but keep their head down and enjoy life, right? Wrong, it wasn't long before Billy found himself back in the sights of the police.

Billy was on bail for over a year whilst the investigation went on regarding the matter of a fraud case worth £30,000 and a red Ferrari. The same make and model as the car Billy had been driving around in.

On the morning of December the 7th 2006 the police came 15 handed to arrest me on a charge involving £30,000 worth of fraud and a Ferrari Testarossa worth 28k. The aggrieved lived in Australia and the bank detail's where the money was paid into was not in my name, the guy in Australia received a badly damaged Ferrari and didn't get his 30k back. this is one thing I didn't do lol I'm sure Jack Daniels wrote the Ferrari off, and god knows who took the 30k lol but like shaggy says 'it wasn't me' lol

They combed my house for a few hours and took my PC which had recently had a new hard drive, some grass cunt called Nick Wilshire, picked me out on an ID parade. They found on picture of a smashed up Ferrari on my PC, but unfortunately for the police when Jack Daniels crashed the car, the plate was lost, so all they had was pics of a Ferrari with no plates on it, shame eh!

Billy Yates

Billy gave no comment for the entire time, documented proof of which is in the letters from his solicitor along with the transcripts of his interview with a CID officer who asked "isn't it a coincidence Mr Martindale that this Ferrari is red the same colour as the Ferrari in question"

I thought 99.9% percent of them are red DUH!!!! But all I could do is smile to myself as I was answering 'no comment' to all his questions.

Billy Yates

Also during that interview it was highlighted that pictures were found on Billy's PC of a smashed Ferrari plus a small picture he had that had Billy leaning out the window of another Ferrari, no number plates were visible, and so they could not know or prove it was the same car.

The next question was a classic, DC Dave then asked me 'isn't it a coincidence William, that the red Ferrari also has the same style wheels on as the one you are pictured with here?' Billy smiled again and answered with 'NO COMMENT'.

Billy Yates

He was interviewed another 3 times during their 12 month affair.

I must say this DC Dave's boss; DS Mayo was a true gent the whole time and didn't go out of his way to be rude or arrogant, as I think he was using my case to train Dave up with.

I am never abusive or rude when I'm arrested as if you are you're just a wanker to yourself, as they just make it harder for you i.e. spit in your tea and take their time questioning you.

Billy Yates

The red Ferrari, which 'Jack Daniels' smashed up

I rang DS Mayo at Epping CID a year to the day I was arrested to see if they had an answer from the CPS, and said 'hello Mr. Mayo, it's our anniversary today' (as it was the 7th of December 2007), and he said 'Bill its good news for you but not for us, it's been declined by the CPS as the main reason was its not in our public interest as the victim lives in Australia, and the evidence the police had was weak. What they know or can prove are two different things'.

DS Mayo is an old school nice copper, he could have been a right bastard, but in my experience, when you're caught your caught. You get nowhere by giving them grief, they're just doing their job and I was doing mine.

Billy Yates

Finally, the need to stop looking over his shoulder had arrived, he could get documentation in his own name and his lifelong desire to legally obtain that drivers licence was now a reality.

I was driving for 17 years with no licence, if I got a pull in a car, I would sell it. I always made sure I had some form of false id in the car, as if you ain't got anything they can keep you in. Churchill insurance was great , as they sent a full policy out straight away, then you cancel it and keep the policy and that would cover you all year, but they stopped all that recently now it's all on DVLA dat's base.

I passed my bike test in May 2007 and car test in June 2007, both first times I might add.

William Martindale

Things were starting to look up for Billy and in tune with his new life; he started to give back to his new community.

The church and its missing roof tiles

The old church Billy and Ian repaired for free when thieves tried to steal 500 roof tiles , the pair of them spent their Sunday putting them all back on, the vicar tried to pay but the lads refused to accept payment.

Handy duo hit the roof after raid by thieves

TWO handy helpers have been praised for their voluntary efforts repairing an ancient church after thieves damaged the roof.

William Martindale, 32, from Cripsey Brook, Ongar, and Ian Radford, 39, from Danes Way, Pilgrims Hatch, decided to take action after seeing that every single tile had been taken off the roof of Beauchamp Roting Church.

Mr Martindale was walking his dog when he saw that the church had been desecrated in the middle of the night.

"I went down in the morning and overnight 500 tiles had been carefully removed from the roof and stacked up next to the church. Every single tile was removed I couldn't believe it. They were obviously planning to come back and pick up the tiles later on."

The 18th Century church has suffered numerous bouts of vandalism over the past year but this was the first time that such an organised attack

Unfortunately for the would-be thieves William contacted his friend Ian, who works for Brentwood-based CBS Builders and the two set about repairing the roof as quickly as possible.

"We spent the next day up on the roof double screwing all the tiles back in place. It's a nice old building and it's so out of the way it is just a target for these kind of attacks. We have already seen the church get vandalised over the past few months we are just trying to keep an eye on it now. It is part of our heritage."

Ian, an avid salsa dancer, even missed his weekly lesson to finish the job.

Rev Tim Pigram said he hoped people would help to keep a watch on his church.

"Over the last year we have had vandalism, probably because it is out of the way but then people were organised and knew what they were doing. It was very nice of Mr Martindale and Mr Radford to help the church like this and

Their exploits hit the local paper

141

Billy also carries out voluntary work helping to rehabilitate youth offenders and wherever possible, raises money for a number of different charities.

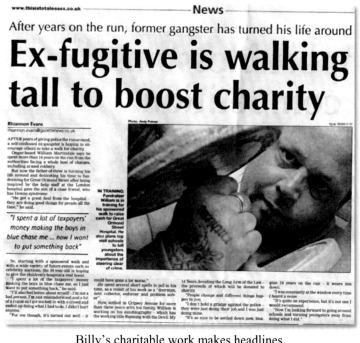

Billy's charitable work makes headlines

Billy is still living in Ongar, Essex with Tina and their three children.

My life has been one big learning curve. I'm not wanted for any crimes now and I'm staying out of trouble. My children are doing really well at school and I want to make sure they don't live the way I have. But I don't regret the things I've done. The people I've hurt are bad people. I've never been a bully. I've only ever bullied bullies.

William Martindale

To help put all his demons to rest, Billy decided he need to air it to anyone and everyone buy writing this book.

It's my life from day one until now. It's been an emotional experience putting it together.

William Martindale

This book hasn't just allowed Billy to put his side out there for others to read, it has also helped him gain a new breed of notoriety which came in handy when an incident involving his older brother Gylnn came about.

My brother Gylnn is a quiet man, he's 40 now and owns his own home and has never had a criminal background, yet we all had the same upbringing. He runs his own business and likes his music; he plays the guitar and in general likes a quiet life.

He purchased a middle floor flat about 6 years ago in Thurrock, Essex, and the flat above is rented, unfortunately a couple moved in who like loud music and big bass speakers and you know how flats are built nowadays, if your neighbour farts you can hear it. So the music was on at all hours and my brother works from home, so at first he ignored it.

He rang me a couple of times for my advice, and my dad's advice, I told him just to go and ask them, 'look do me a favour please and keep the music down as I work from home and its shaking my place to bits'. So he did and they agreed but the music carried on and this went on for a few weeks. Don't get me wrong, even though my brother likes a calm life he does not suffer fools and has a nasty temper which he loses really quickly if aggravated, it must be passed down from dad lol.

Then one night he had reached boiling point, they were jumping up and down on the floor with the music banging, he rang me and said 'I'm going up there', and could I come over and watch his back as it was obvious there was a small party going on and a few of them up there. I advised him not to go up there alone as I couldn't get to him, but he had had enough.

I sent big Paul Meeking over to his to watch his back; Paul jumped in his car and was there in 20 minutes. They then knocked on the door and the fella or one of the fella's came to the door and said 'we're having a party mate, what's ya problem?' to which a 40ish year old man came from out the door toward by brother and said 'what you gonna do about it?'

He was moving towards my brother, so my brother threw a peach of a right hand (crack) and sent him back through the doorway with teeth flying here and there, splitting the fella's lip about an inch long up to his nose. The fella got to his feet, obviously been sniffing shit and drinking and a scuffle ensued.

Paul broke it up and the neighbour called the police, I told my brother to go to mine and wait for me, I said just grab some clothes and go as fast as you can, so he did. When I got home he was a bit scratched and bruised but that didn't matter as he had clearly done the fella, he lost 4 teeth in total with one right hand, another thing we learnt from dad.

The next day, just in case he had a little firm plotted up in waiting for my brother, I got a couple of pals together, big Paul Meeking, Ian Radford, Roy Shaw and me and went to the flat to collect some of my brothers things.

Roy just wanted to rip someone's head off and quickly offered to come along for the ride. As we pulled up out of the flats, in the small car park which is overlooked by most of the flats, we all got out of the car, Roy jumped out of the back shouting 'come on you cunts, where are ya, lets fucking have ya' I'm like, 'Roy, calm down mate, we're just here in case of any trouble, we don't wanna attract too much attention'. so Ian waited by the car and me, Paul and Roy went upstairs to the flat and that was it, Roy's off again on the stairs shouting 'where is the cunt' at the top of his voice.

So we're now in the flat collecting Glynn's shoes and clothing, bits and bobs and Roy starts jumping up and down in the middle of Glynn's front room singing "come on" "come on, come on, come on" his old fighting song, at the top of his voice, we did laugh though as Roy just wanted a fight. It shows even at 72 he still wants it lol, then that's what Roy is like, when he's on ya side and if he likes you that week lol. In the car, Roy sighed and said 'bollocks I was looking forward to a ruck there'.

I dropped my card in the pricks letterbox with the picture of my book cover on it and my website address, phone number, email and all that and wrote 'call, it's for the best'.

low and behold, they must have looked on my website and realised whose brother they fucked with, I received a call that morning apologising over and over again, saying 'look he's lost four teeth, please don't get involved Billy, we didn't realise he was your brother', I said 'he didn't need me anyway he's been done fair and square and if anything happens to him or his car, I will be round'.

The music has never been on since.

Billy Yates

Not only has having a book and a website etc depicting who you are been favourable for Billy, it has also opened up a new world of friends and supporters, amongst whom, are in the following section:

To my true friend Billy Yates,

"You cannot choose your battlefield--God will do that for you, but you can fly your flag where no flag ever flew.

I wrote that poem with you in mind Billy... as I think it sums you in many ways. I am looking forward to visiting England and meeting you at long last... as from what I have read and heard about you ...you are one of England's true hard men... a dying breed in a modern day world that has lost its guts and dash....in a world where a man's word can no longer be counted on and his hand shake believed in.........

All the best mate, your friend always.

Mark Brandon "Chopper" Read

Our dear friend Billy, whom has become a very close friend to us both over six months now of regular calls, a new found friendship that we welcome and treasure, we look forward in meeting you one day and hopefully you and Mark could work the circuit together and spread your stories across and make a million.

There lots of pebbles on the sand, but there are only a few that may shine in a lifetime and I guess you're one of those few.

All the best your book launch and hope it makes number one (well I guess it will now, since I'm in it hah hah)

To a great guy with a great sense of humour, love and Best wishes.

Margaret Read

Mark and Margaret Read on their wedding day

Me and mark have become good friends over the phone, the papers have done an article on the both of us and how we are similar in many ways. He's had a raw deal from people, ripping him off for money; he didn't get a penny for his film, or his Chopper beer brand, some dog used him again. His shows are great and he sends me books, over 50 photos, DVDs of his shows, he has asked me to do his security when he gets here. I'm going over to him early next year to stay with him and his wife, Margaret, she is a lovely woman, and we talk for hours on the phone too. I have sent him pictures of me and my family and friends, and a signed 'pretty boy' book and a signed book 'wild thing' of my dad's.

We chat about day to day things like the weather and the little differences between England and Oz. I can't wait to see him and Margaret, its great when he calls as we talk for hours.

William Martindale

Roy Shaw, Billy Frost and Billy

I first met Billy on the Trisha Goddard show, I found him a very interesting person and I took a liking to him straight away, we got to talking about different people and I found we knew some of the same people.

Billy was on the run for 16 years, I think this was quite a feat, I was on the run for 9 years myself so I know how hard it can be.

I have met Billy twice since then; I went to the opening of a pub where I met Billy and Roy Shaw, I then went with Billy and a friend, Lenny Hamilton out to a pub crawl around some lovely villages, we had a good day.

I wish Billy lots of luck with his book, which I am sure will be a good one, good luck Billy.

Billy Frost

I first met Bill Yates when we did the Trisha show together with Billy Frost. I must say that Bill Yates spoke a lot of sense while we were on the Trisha Godard show a few weeks ago.

Me and Billy Frost then went to have a few drinks with him where he lives in Ongar Essex. Me and Frosty had a lovely day out with Billy Yates as we visited some lovely country pubs. As the day went on I could see that Billy Yates is quite well known all over Essex and it was my pleasure to meet up with him again because he showed us and gave us a great day out so god bless Mr. Yates I think that you are a 22 carat man.

Lenny Hamilton

I don't know Billy that well but I have heard he has a 'don't give a monkeys' attitude, and he's like his father in many ways, and his father has a very powerful reputation. I speak with Billy on the phone occasionally, and a good kid polite and respectful, I wish him all the best with the book.

Freddy Foreman

Steve and me have been pals for over a year now and I must say he's one of the last old school doormen. We have seen a little action a few times and has been big Paul's employer for a while. Steve is my pal and a true gentleman, one real old school fella; Steve had known of me through certain people and shows nothing but respect to me and my pals including Roy Shaw. A true gent thanks Steve.

William Martindale

Steve and Billy

Jason, Paul and Billy at the Sugar Hut, Brentwood

Jason the traveller, money maker, 100% diamond fella, him and his brother, Johnny. The first time I met Jason, I was involved in a 10 mile car chase, after 2 black fella's tried to rob Jason's pals. We were on the wrong side of the road doing 120 MPH in Jason's £150k '08 plate Bentley Cabriolet. We caught them in the end and Jason respects me for my loyal part in this.

William Martindale

I have known Billy now for over a year and in that time we have become very close friends. I feel lucky to have Billy as a friend because I know how hard it is for him to trust somebody enough from them to get close to him and it is a shame because Billy has so much more to offer than what people perceive he is generous, very funny and very very loyal.

I know if I had a problem and needed help he would think nothing of driving the hundreds of miles from London to Newcastle to help me and not even want a thanks for doing it.

Billy has had a very eventful life and his close friends read as a who's who of the British underworld so I don't even have to wish him luck for the release of his book as I know without a doubt it will be a best seller.

With the release of the book people will see another side to Billy Martindale and hopefully it's the start of better things to come for him.

To sum up Billy in a few words as the Londoners say, 100% diamond geezer, Billy I am proud to call you my friend.

Michael `Nezzy` Nesbitt

Nezzy is a diamond and a man you can trust 100%, he has helped me and my dad so so much, he's a proper human being, and we speak on the phone most nights. No man has a bad word to say about him. Thanks Nezzy mate.

William Martindale

Michael 'Nezzy' Nesbit and Frankie Fraser outside Turnmills nightclub

Billy boy is a real gentleman and a good person to chat to, I look forward to Billy's book and I'm pleased by the way Billy has looked after Roy Shaw in recent times. Billy thinks the world of Roy even though they do fall out once a week, I think Billy deserves all the luck in the world. I'm also very good friends with Michael Nesbitt and I wish Billy all the best.

Frankie Fraser

I've only known Billy a short while but find him to be very loyal to his friends.

If you are honest with him and tell him how it is he will treat you the same way. He's not a person I would like to meet in a dark alley at night but he is the person I would

want with me in the trenches. Treat him with respect and you'll see the good side of Billy Boy. Treat him badly and you are in trouble.

Phil Howard

Billy with Phil Howard

To this day I still have enemies from the criminal world that are out there, waiting for their opportunity to get me but there is one I have vowed to eliminate. He hides away behind his computer and mobile phone, I won't name and shame this man but it will soon be evident who this coward is, he was/is hell bent on destroying my book and good reputation. I think this man just wants to fuck me, more in a sexual way than a violent one lol I'm not at all worried about this sick perverted individual, he has threatened to rape my wife and kids and kill me. The shit cunt lives in hiding, as most people want a pop at him, no doubt I will be questioned when he is found dead somewhere. Then we can have a great fucking party!!!!

Billy Yates

I love my Dad and he's still my hero. It's a real pity Roy Shaw never fought Dad, when Dad was fit, as Dad would of done Roy easily, and Roy knows it. Most of Roy's fights were fixed; Roy stayed well clear of my Dad and never frequented the clubs my Dad worked at. My Dad challenged Roy at every chance and Roy declined.

William Martindale

Roy and Lew have been good mates for over 30 years

There you have it, Billy's life summed up for all to read, digest and debate.

Be sure to check out his website:

www.billyboymartindale.com

And his father's site:

http://www.lewwildthingyates.com

In the worst of us is the best of us! Billy boy Martindale

With all that's been said, I thought it only fitting to give Lew the final word.

Billy and his Dad, Lew

We have had a love hate relationship over the years but he is my son and I love him.

I really don't know why over the years he has rebelled so much but with the naughty bad side of him there is a good side, kind, funny and very loving, I feel in my heart what it is, is that he needs to be wanted.

Lew `wild thing` Yates

THE AUTHORS

Paul is a 100% individual a proper private and a hard hard person to work out; I have met many people in my life but not like him.... He likes his mind games and can get into people's heads and organise a five aside football match....

He baffle's me but all the rows we have had I still like him , without Paul I wouldn't have this book or met all my new friends inc Jamie, Mark Emmins and Chopper Read, he has changed my life and I thank him for that, and I can now make wicked mint sauce x

William Martindale

Paul Knight and Billy

What can I say about Billy that anyone who just read about his life would believe? This salt of the earth that is respected by big some big names within the criminal fraternity and everyone that has known him, talks about respect, one of ya own, a diamond geezer. But to me, Billy Yates is an utter cunt, pure and simple. He is a ball of fury that does bully the weak and defenceless, alienates people and has to play childish games to get his own way. It was Billy Yates that had me walk away from this book; it was originally going to be a fully detailed journey into his exploits whilst on the run. I had written 75% of it already when I had had enough of his behaviour and bully by tactics towards me and deleted it. Just how many times can you be called a 'cunt' and still laugh it off? Just how are you meant to react when you are branded a 'fucking nonce, mongrel grass'? Threats of wanting to bury you? Abusive voicemails and constant calls which reached the point of almost having to change your number because personal boundaries and common decency cannot be understood or respected, how many times can you let that behaviour slide because it is all blamed on drink? No, to me, Billy Yates embodies everything he tells the world he hates, a hypocrite to the fullest extent, a bully and a publicity seeking parasite that will use and abuse any and all in his way.

Billy (William) Martindale on the other hand, is one of the funniest, friendliest, larger than life personalities you'll ever have the pleasure of meeting. This is the guy that apologised to me, admitting his faults and flaws to get me to produce an honest account as to why the animal that is Billy Yates came about. A man full of insecurities that wants to trust those that try to help him the most, a man with limitations that undermines himself and disbelieves his own capabilities away from a world of survival. I came back to this project for two reasons, I still believed that his story had to be told, even if it seems more summarised than in-depth and secondly, I wanted to force Billy to produce most of this story about himself. To motivate and encourage him

158

to stop depending on Yates and have Martindale take him to new places. It was after completing his involvement in this book that Billy is now considering penning another book about his experiences on the door and with the realms of security and debt collecting. I wish him all the best on that venture.

I have to agree with my pal Jamie O'Keefe when he says that although Billy can leave you with a negative impression, give the guy another chance. He knows where he has gone wrong and is attempting to change his outlook and make the most of the new opportunities that are forever presenting themselves to him. If you still think that the beast is still lurking within, then drop him, go away shouting 'I told you so!'

He hasn't had an easy life; he has had to face a number of issues that most people never have to encounter once. He is what he is, a product of his own environment that has had to endure and sacrifice more than he'll ever let on.

Billy Martindale is my friend and I'm glad I could help him get a jump start into something new. My only hope is that he'll continue to pursue all that he wishes to succeed in his life and not let the nay sayers have him revert back to the person that makes others feel better about themselves as they condemn and categorise Billy as a no hope, waste of space living off the name and fame of others. He's better than that; I just don't think he knows it yet.

Paul Knight

Jamie knows me so well its untrue, he says in me he sees himself when he was young, and I remind him of his oldest son, Jamie. He has helped me save my life, and it's always a great pleasure to talk to him when he rings, I think secretly he would love me as a neighbour, so I could bring him bakewell tarts. A quiet man but definitely no mug

William Martindale

Jamie O'Keefe and Billy

I remember the first day I met Billy. I had just come from hospital after having a physical encounter the night before. I had one arm battered and bruised which I couldn't use so my youngest son Adam was driving me, my back was injured from grappling around on the pavement, and I was carrying a bag of anti HIV/Aids medication that I had been issued due to being bitten so hard on the face that the teeth went through all 7 layers of skin. So I wasn't in the best shape or frame of mind for a meeting, but Billy was introduced to my publishing company by Paul Knight, so it was only right that I took some time out to meet him.

We arranged to meet in a local cafe in Dagenham to discuss his book. I hobbled into the cafe and Bill was already there. I didn't know what he looked like but I saw this heavily tattooed, shaved headed, lump with his two phones. Didn't take too much working out. Within a few minutes of chatting, he was on his phone wheeling and

160

dealing with car sales talk. In-between that, he was trying to find out what I had been involved in the night before and was telling me his war stories from his book.

I knew nothing at all about Bill other than his dad was the well known unlicensed fighter Lew Yates. The main thing I liked about Billy was that he was funny. Very funny. It also came across clearly that he was very proud of his dad and wanted to be respected in the same way. He reminded me so much of my oldest son Jamie and that enabled me to see further than the person that Billy was presenting to me. I was seeing a lovable rouge but with some hidden issues that were affecting him.

From that day on I got to know Billy very well. I even took him to Cambridge to record the interviews he did with the travellers and to get more insight into the murder of his mate Tommy, and I took photos at the graveyard and with Tommy's parents. So where possible, I went to verify some of the stories in Billy's book and also took photographic evidence and newspaper reports. As time went on I found Billy to be hilarious with some of the pranks he would get up to and that was the side of him that I found appealing. The down side to this was that I soon realized that Billy didn't understand boundaries. If you ask him to not phone you after 9pm, he would still think nothing of phoning you from 10pm through to 2-3am the next morning and would call you dozens of times throughout that period. Even when I ignored the calls he would withhold his number or use different phones to call. That side of our friendship, I did not like, and it forced me to distance myself from Billy for a while and I saw him less and less in person. I didn't dislike him and we have never fallen out but I felt smothered. But in the back of my mind Billy still reminded me so much of my wayward son who as an adult is still looking for acceptance but just didn't understand how to behave with different people at different levels.

Billy just wanted friendship but I don't think he understood how to treat people or how to react to situations that made him feel uncomfortable. If you speak to Bill you will see that he is very well spoken, can hold a conversation, and has a side to him that enjoys listening to Classical music and visiting old Castles and stately homes and studying nature, but that is tarnished at times by a side of him that makes you not want to be in the same room as him. So from my time of meeting Billy to now, I had to distance myself from him in order to allow us to remain friends. I have always been honest with Billy and pointed out his good and bad points and have always encouraged him to do better for himself. Whenever I speak to Billy now he still never fails to make me laugh, and I do try to be as understanding as I can when he is having a day of throwing his toys out the pram. I think Billy unknowingly has managed to disassociate himself with a lot of people through not thinking about the knock on affect of his actions at times, but the Billy I have seen of late is someone who is trying to make positive change.

If you have crossed paths with Bill and it has left you with a negative impression of him, give him a chance to show he is making positive change. If he still hasn't changed, in your opinion, then you will know that it's not a friendship that is going to work.

I like Bill but I wouldn't want him as a neighbour. My neighbours understand boundaries and I think it's something Billy still needs to work on. To finish off, I would like to say that I have seen a side of Billy that shows he has a heart of Gold, but it goes unnoticed when he does something else that destroys the good gesture. I remember one day we had spent the day at Roy Shaw's house and afterwards we went to a local pub to have a chat. Billy had ordered me a meal and refused to let me pay for it. I think the bill for both of us came to about £30. Billy insisted on paying for it.

Later on I found out that Billy only had £40 on him to last the week and £30 of that went on the meal. That's the kind and thoughtful side of Billy that you don't always get a chance to see. Then there's the prankster side to Billy where he asked me to pop over his house with my son so he can fix my lads car as a favour, in the process he asked me if I like Crayfish, which I do. He then took us to the river at the back of his house and pulled out a Crayfish trap with a single Crayfish in it. "Here you go mate, it's yours", total madness. That's the funny side of Billy. We let it go. Another time I was on my way out one day and I got a call from Billy "Jamie, when I was in your car earlier I put my house key in your sun visor, can you check it's there as I'm locked out". I was driving so pulled down the visor and got covered in crumbled up cake. Billy had planted a Bakewell Tart there and broke it up so it would go all over me. I had it in my eyes, all over my face and clothes and I was on my way to a meeting. That's the funny side of Bill that I like.

So that's my opinion of Billy boy Martindale-Yates and I hope you can form your own opinion of Billy from meeting him yourself and reading his book rather than taking on someone else's second hand opinion. I wish him well with his book and in life.

Jamie O'Keefe

Jamie sent me this story below and I believe never a truer word has been spoken.

William Martindale

One evening an old Cherokee told his grandson about a battle that goes on inside people.

He said, 'My son, the battle is between 'two wolves' inside us all.

'One is Evil. It is anger, envy, jealousy, sorrow, regret, greed, arrogance, self-pity, guilt, resentment, inferiority, lies, false pride, superiority, and ego.'

'The other is Good. It is joy, peace, love, hope, serenity, humility, kindness, benevolence, empathy, generosity, truth, compassion and faith.'

The grandson thought about it for a minute and then asked his grandfather, 'Which wolf wins?' The old Cherokee simply replied, 'The one you feed.'

A Motivational Story with Wisdom - Two Wolves

Cherokee Wisdom

Interview by Jamie O'Keefe

Bill, I have spent many hours chatting to you, and have captured you on tape and video talking about some of the things that have happened in your life. I know you have shared your story within this book so just to give a bit more insight into the events and your feelings in general, I would like to run the following questions by you.

You mentioned that at one time that a contract of sorts was set up for someone to kill you, can you tell us more about that?

It was at the time of me robbing the drug dealers. I can't prove it but I had done this dealer for about £17,000 and at the same time I find out that this dealer is connected to this Jason who set me up. Maybe just a coincidence but this Jason phones me to offer me a debt collection. I had to meet someone at the local garages to meet someone. I was parked up at these garages on Lyons Farm, round the back of these garages. I got a phone call. This Jason, fucking proper set me up. Erm, he was paid money to go and have me killed or set me up to have me killed and I was waiting round the garages and erm if I, I said I'll meet you round there but as I, I was a bit suspicious, I'm always a bit paranoid and I was sticking to one side of the garages as this car come round it was a VW Passat, yeah a big Passat thing and erm, as I'm there at the first garage door, if I'd of been at the second one I would of been dead. But as the car pulled round I've seen the car. I went, "alright mate," I know there was two other geezers in the back and the back window open as well as the front window and the fucking barrel just come out the window. I grabbed at the gun and I pulled it to one side, the gun's gone off up the inside of me forearm, the powder burn has done my arm, the fucking blast has hit the garage door, which you can see pictures of and I've got powder burns and shit and skin all fucking flaking off me arms and blood everywhere but I wasn't actually shot. I wasn't actually done with a pellet. I might have been grazed by a couple but it was a bit of a burn, mess, well burn, bloody burnt and everything and all pussy and that. Erm and I fucking pulled the gun from his hands. I actually had the gun out of his hands and it was only a single barrel and I fucking launched the gun at the car bounced off the back of the motor, this car spun off like that and that was it. And then I went and got some tools and we looked for 'em. And that was when I got shot, or shot at. Err that's pretty much how it happened mate.

You said you worked in Stratford and met a good friend, who was that?..

It was a fella called Chris Donnelly in Wheeler's Nightclub in Stratford when I was working the door with Rob and Lee. Chris looks a bit like the one out of Snatch with the flattish nose and dark hair, rough looking. He'd just not long got out of prison because him and his dad had a row with some geezer in a pub in Stratford and Chris cut him with a Stanley blade across the back and severed his spinal cord. Got involved with Chris. We done a few blags and that, robbed drug dealers. But we were running out of drug dealers and I had to find more contacts and more people all the time to find out where there were more dealers to earn more money. There was eventually a shortage of drug dealers or ones that had enough money that was significant enough to rob. It's not worth turning over a drug dealer if he's only got five, six hundred quid. So yeah, that's where I met Chris. It was time to leave Chris when he stabbed someone up really bad. This wasn't with me or anything to do with me or the work I was doing. I was pretty much anti-knife, if we was doing anything it would be with guns. I don't know if that's any better but, who gives a fuck anyway. That's what we did. So yeah Chris stabbed someone up pretty bad, I'm not even sure he got caught about it but that was the last time really I had much to do with him. I spoke to him recently but he's gone

166

off the rails now, his dad had a stroke years ago, ended up in a wheelchair, and its affected him, he's just been pissed all the time since. He's just got out of rehab now. I spoke to him two days after he got out of rehab and he's out of his nut on fucking Skull Super lager, you know Super Tenants and all that shit. So you know, I won't bother with him. If he doesn't wanna help himself you can't help someone like that. It's the same as what you've been trying to do for you sister all these years. Until she is ready to come of the booze and the gear, you can't really help her.

What do you think the turning point was for you in going straight?

Probably when I moved back home with Tina, went to work for a guy in Romford. He had a car site and he offered me a job. He said, "I'll give you a hundred and fifty pound a week basic and a hundred pound a car." So I was ok. This was importing cars from Japan. This is when it first started to come big in this country. It was about '96, '97 people were bringing over Pajero's and all the Japanese sports cars like Skylines and the Subaru's and you know. Same as what you did with that Izuzu you brought over from Japan. We was sort of bringing 'em over from ages ago. So he offered me a job, £150 basic and a hundred pound a car. First week I took seven hundred fifty quid. I sold seven cars and one hundred and fifty basic and regular, worst week I had there was about five hundred quid. I was earning so much money. Done really well. Then the geezer got a bit greedy, not greedy so much but he wanted to cut my money down so I said to him, "well I'm selling the cars, I'm running the site, locking it up, opening it up in the morning." You know, all right he give me choice of cars to go round in.I could choose whichever I wanted which was quite nice. This was the time when I got on the path to being more straight for the time being. After working there for six months I'd went and been and bought myself an R1 motorbike, nearly new, nearly new R1. All the leathers and all the racing gear flying around with my mates. Friend of mine bought a Ducati; his name was Mick, from Southend. Erm, Ducati 911 motorbike. He bought it off a guy who'd dropped it and the guy was in a wheelchair, he broke his back. So he bought it of him and he fixed it back up, got it on the road. And we was out one day at High Beach, we was coming back from High Beach coming through the lanes towards, Theydon Bois. We're all in front, he's, Mick's trying to catch up apparently what's happened is a car has been like just poodling along and he's, we've all gone round this car, he's took it on a bend, on a left-hand bend or coming into a left-hand bend and he's clipped the front of the car where he's tried to cut in because there was a car coming the other side of the road. Anyway he's clipped it or, he's just caught it with his back wheel, the back end of the bike and he come off, the bike slid off into the trees, into the bushes, and he survived, he's in the middle of the road and as he was getting up on one knee, a car come round and killed him. He was just getting up off the floor and the car come round, blind bend, smash, dead. So he died and that was sad cause I'd known him for you know a couple of years, three or four years maybe. Before hand we used to take the cars up down to Southend and cruise round and pick up the odd bird and that, you know, years ago. Yeah it was a shame what happened to him. You know I've lost three or four friends now on bikes.

After that I just you know, hung round with a few friends. It put me off the bike, really. I didn't wanna ride it for a few months. I put it away in me shed and didn't really want to use it too much. I did, it come out again and I started using it again. Riding with a fella from over Chelmsford. At this time I was going clubbing with Roy. Used to go to the country club with Roy years ago. Went back home to Vines Close in Dagenham, that's where I lived with Tina. She fell pregnant with Lewis, and Lewis is now ten.
That was a good feeling, a very good feeling, you know, I'll never forget the day he was born, still picture it now, you know the minute he was born. That was in '98 after Princess

*Diana died. . I know everyone remembers where they were
when that happened. At that time I did have a room in Forest
Gate as well, that I'd flit backwards and forward to no
matter where, even if I was staying back with Tina I always
had a spare place on the side so I could just leave and go
straight back to you know, my place, if the Old Bill turned up*

When did you start messing with guns?

*Well dad used to go away and leave me with a gun quite
often a twelve bore, a four ten shotgun and we'd blow holes
in everything. . He'd come back and he'd say basically
when he went, anyone hanging around son, you know, fire a
shot up in the air or two above their heads, you know like
over their heads and they'll soon piss off you know. So, no
one ever hung around and I just shot holes in every bloody
thing I could find. Dad went mental when he come home and
there's holes in all these big drums he had to keep for
something but I just blew everything away and everything got
shot, you know. I was twelve years old you know. Who in
their right mind, I mean fuck me, I would never do that for
my twelve year old. Wouldn't leave him with a bloody
gatgun let alone a bloody shotgun. But erm, I don't know
what he was doing. So he must've trusted me to some extent.
Me and Darren used to have airguns and we'd fire them
everywhere and dad would come home and sit in his
armchair and he'd look up and he'd think what the fuck's
that in my ceiling and there'd be all pellets in there what we
shot in the ceiling, me and Nobby.*

What you been up to recently?

*I did a job a few weeks ago with triple X Paul, we have
worked a few doors together such as the Cauliflower Ilford,
Eastside, Eva Hart, and as another earner we do debt
collecting together. There was this fella who owed about
£4,000 who didn't want to pay. We paid him a visit and I
took out his car windows out and smashed the bodywork with*

a baseball bat and Paul stabbed up the tyres etc while the guy watched from indoors. We then drove away with the lights off and parked up to make our call to him. Thanks to Argos, you can get a mobile phone that's untraceable for £14.99 so we did that and called him. The only down side to that is that you can't return it within the 14 days for a refund (laughs) but we got the money a few days later. £4,014.99 (laughs).

It was even funnier when we went to get some beers from Tesco and celebrate our earner. Paul was in the queue carrying the bulk of the booze and I've loaded him up even more. He is doing the macho thing making out that he isn't struggling but I could see the veins popping out his neck and his blood pressure going to the top floor. I grabbed hold of his track suit bottoms and pants and pulled then to his ankles. He was standing there holding cases of beer with his cock on show. Fucking hilarious. He then hobbled along like a penguin to the conveyor belt and dropped the beers on the counter to pull up his bottoms. Priceless!

It's not the first time I've done him like that. Once he was up a ladder when we were replacing roof tiles on a local church that some chavy bastards had stolen. He was up the ladder and he got his kit pulled down by me again. That's what I like about him, he can take a joke.

Once when he was round my house I crept out and put Gaffa tape over the back and sides of his car where he couldn't see it and wrote on the tape in big letters 'Sex case'. He drove from my house down the M25 in busy traffic to his mothers in Barking without knowing. People were driving past and shouting out things like 'you fucking nonce, kiddy fiddler etc' which he isn't, so can you imagine how freaked out he was. He had only just bought the car so thought it must have belonged to a wrongun. He got to his mums and still didn't know and phoned me ' Bill I've got to get shot of this fucking car, you never guess what just happened to me?', by this time his mother had been outside for a smoke and came back in ' What's all that writing on that car about Sex Case?'.

All I heard was 'Bill you cunt' as I'm pissing myself laughing. He is a good laugh. He is such a good mate and would get out of bed and come and get me in Scotland if I had broken down. He is 100% and I can't thank him enough for his friendship. As you know I am really hard to put up with at times and he has always put up with my shit. He is one in a million, such a lovely fella! Thanks XXXPaul.

I know you're an animal lover Bill so I found it a bit strange that you worked at that Animal testing place in Cambridge?

It wasn't like that. I wasn't anything to do with animal testing, more like people testing. There was no animal testing going on then it was just a new build up on the M11 that had different people building and constructing the thing. I was working for this really nice guy chlorinating the water systems. I think his name was Andrew Lambert and he was paying me £500 a week to work for him there as a water engineer!. But soon after this horrible cunt Mark threw some money into the business and took over as my boss, or so he thought. He was a right cocky cunt and tried treating me like a fucking mug so I treated him to a lump of 4x2 across his face and took all his front teeth out, then stamped all over him. It cost him about £4,500 to have the teeth redone. So after I smashed his face I knew I wasn't going to get paid so I fucked off with his company van and fuel card. I diesel-ed up everyone I knew in Cambridge on his fuel card. It came to a right load of money and he eventually phoned me and asked how we can resolve it. I exchanged the fuel card for the vans logbook. Seemed like a fair swap to me as the van was only 3 years old (laughs). Fuck him the horrible cunt, but give him his due, he didn't grass me up to the old bill so I give him credit for that.

What about training, have you moved away from that now?

No I still keep my hand in but obviously not to the same degree as I did when I was a kid. I've got a gym at the bottom of my garden and have just bought floor to ceiling balls, heavy bags, and I do a lot of weight now. As I get older I'm not getting lighter or thinner so I have changed my training to accommodate my build. I'm more into power now and want to hit hard and puff and blow less. It seems to work better for me that,plus I'm being honest with myself and not trying to kid myself that I can go the distance like I could as a kid. If I can deal with a situation quickly its better for me. Like when those three wankers tried it at Leytonstone for no reason at all as I'm walking along with Tina minding my own fucking business. One of them bumps into me like that guy in the Verve video. I'm thinking what the fuck is that all about and Tina knows it's gonna go off. As I've looked at him the three try fucking intimidating me. I've seen this game plan before where some poor cunt gets robbed and stabbed up coz he is thinking more about protecting his missus. I did the three of them there and then with ammonia, cunts, they didn't expect that. I got a mate who is a chemist and he gets me bits and pieces and this ammonia was the fucking full on stuff.

So are you bit of a tough guy that hangs out with villains then?

Not at all, I'm just a normal guy like you Jay'm, but if it comes knocking at my door I will fucking deal with it. I'm not trying to say I'm a fucking angel but I just like a quiet life and am content sitting indoors listening to Mozart and other classical music and being a parent. BUT... I do have to earn a living and do lose my temper at times and its incidents that involve those two things that don't leave me with the best of reputations. But I don't drive about listening to all that gangster rap and giving it large to people that can't look after themselves. Any cunt can do that. And when you see me in pictures holding guns and stuff, I'm just taking the piss out of those cunts that think they are gangsters. Like these silly fucking chavs kids who think they run the show. They are fucking idiots.

I hate the chavy teenage kids we see now. I like nice polite kids that you can look at that wanna do something for themselves. I know it makes me bit of a hypocrite considering my past but it's the mistakes that I've made that make me not want to see the same in my kids and their generation.

BILLY ON AN OLD VESPA
SCOOTER AT FOREST GATE
ABOUT 1983

When I was a kid I played with old Scooters/bikes and learnt about them, not fucking knives and drugs. When I had dogs they were my best friend, not a fucking chavy status symbol. I know you have a lovely Staffie that you love to death but these silly Essex boys walking the street with their Staffies and other dogs another tool of theirs, makes me sick. Look at your kids jay'm, you brought them up as a lone parent just as my dad did and it's hard to keep track. He worked the doors as you did and did his best to provide us with everything. But things that are out of a parents control

sometimes take over and I ended up wayward as your eldest boy Jamie did. I'm not being disrespectful, as I know you won't mind me saying this. But your other kids have all come out sound as have my siblings. But we each had the same upbringing. But these chavy cunts you see today are just gang wanabee bad boys who don't want to do anything for

173

themselves. They are scum. With their fucking silly back to front baseball caps, trousers down to their arse and silly fucking attitude. White boys that wannabe black. Fucking makes me sick. If a black boy wants to identify with his roots and show it off in the way he bowls about, I can understand that as long as it's without the fucking attitude. You know, attitude where attitude is deserved but attitude 24/7 as a fucking act is just bollocks. Even my mate Neil who is black says that they fucking hate these white boys trying to talk and act like the proper black guys do. Neil Charles was the mate I used to work with robbing the drug dealers, we hated the cunts.

I would like to just get away from it all with the missus and the kids to a remote valley or hillside where there is nobody else is around and sit by a pool listening to my favourite piece 'Marriage of Figaro' which means 'Crazy day' and pretty much describes most of my days. Yeah that would do me.

So why don't you do that then?

Well I was hoping that by now I would have pissed off enough people and everyone would have moved away leaving me living alone in Essex, but it hasn't worked out like that yet (laughs)

But seriously, I don't like Cities, crowds, the underground system, but I do like the old buildings in London, I'm into history. I'm a member of 'English Heritage' and go see things like Osborne house on the Isle of White, Bodiam Castle in East Sussex, Kent. It was built around 1386 based on the design of the French Castles of that time. So copycat counterfeiting was going on even then (laughs). But if I went on youtube talking about Castles and Mozart then nobody would wanna read my book. All that mouthing and cunting off like I do on those youtube clips is just an advert. You know that anyway, you filmed it. But that's the media bookselling Billy, not the Billy sitting here today talking to you. I'm not saying that I'm not like that as well because you know I am. But that's just one side of me and it really depends on how I

174

take someone's attitude towards me that decides on my reaction. I don't plan it, I just react. It's like when you suddenly touch something that burns you, there is no plan. You just react and nothing can stop that. But I think I'm reasonable cultured for someone that's been on the run and had a past of crime. I've been bit of a tearaway. Oh one thing, I fucking hate football and don't do politics. So that's two things I don't get involved in. Talk to me about football and I'm gone. Fucking hate it.

Anything else you don't like?

I hate jealous selfish two faced people. I hate it when you tell someone something and they go and tell someone else out of spite or jealousy rather that in a positive way. That's one thing I really admire about you. You are arrogant and rude at times but you are always honest. If you don't like something I've done you will tell me but if you think I've done something good, you will tell me. You are straight with me and the main thing about you is you cannot be bought. You have proved that to me on more than one occasion and that's rare. If you said to me 'Bill, if you do such and such – I will never have contact with you again' I know that you will follow that through. You do something if you say you are going to do it. That's why everyone knows where they stand with you. But I will tell someone they are a cunt, a mongrel, a nonce etc and I will never speak to them again, but the following day we are chatting again. I suppose I forgive people whereas you don't. My point is that you never show jealousy, selfishness or say something about someone that you haven't or wouldn't say to them. I also tell people what I feel about them but it always ends up getting nasty.
But real two faced people don't get a second chance with me, thats it, they are gone and I've lost a lot of friends that way. But sometimes people can't control how they act because of illness or emotional shit that takes over their mind so they deserve a second chance even if they have wronged you.

Give me an example Bill?

This one is funny but serious at the same time. I was out with Roy (Shaw) one day at the Bull in Fyfield as he had been feeling a bit low as the doctor had put him on medication for memory loss and just needed to sit with a mate and not feel he was losing it. We had a good day and I left him in the afternoon as he had to meet up with his ex Caroline, mother of his kids Tina and Gary. Anyway I gets a call from him the next day ' Bill you bastard, what were you doing in my garden last night, fucking playing with my daughters tits right in front of me' I was thrown back for a second ' Roy what the fuck are you talking about, you've lost it now, what the fuck you on about'. But there was no reasoning with him 'Roy phone me back when you're normal' and I put the phone down. I didn't know what was going on as I wasn't anywhere near the party the night before in Collier Row. I think it was his daughters 40th birthday or something and I hadn't seen her for about 10 years so fuck knows what he was on about. I stewed over it for about half an hour and thought 'fuck this' I've got to find out what this is all about, so phoned him back. As he is still cunting me off I'm trying to find out what it was all about. 'Roy, Tina just got married about a month ago, maybe you saw her with someone else but it fucking wasn't me'. And I put the phone down. So on the Sunday, two days after the party he phones me again ' Bill, She has fucking smashed my car up, Tina's done my car' I said 'don't be silly Roy, why would she do that?', he said that he had also phoned his daughter and said ' You slag, you dirty fucking whore, stealing my money and letting Bill play with your tits' so she got it all off him as well, for no reason and must have been as confused as I was.

I said 'Roy, don't be so pathetic, how the fuck can you talk to your daughter like that, and I've got my missus here, what's going on'

Anyway to cut a long story short it turned out that he wasn't allowed to drink alcohol on the tablets the doctor gave him. I checked the info on the meds he was on and it said 'must not be taken with alcohol, can cause irritability, mood swings, hallucinations and a bit of other stuff. Basically it should have said 'Do not ever give this medication to Roy Shaw'. It was the worst thing he could have taken on top of all the booze he had that day. He isn't the calmest of people on a good day so to have that sort of cocktail is like a time bomb. He spoke to his ex Caroline and found out that his daughter Tina wasn't even at the party and was at home with her husband all weekend, I also wasn't there so it was all in his mind. All I can think is that he thought about the two people that wasn't there and his medication and booze made him to hallucinate a load of shit, which became real for him.

But with that all solved and him realising what the meds had done to him it starts making him paranoid. His car was smashed up but it wasn't Tina, someone had obviously hit it or a tree or bit of street furniture had bashed the car up, so he asked me to go sort his blown tyre.Bearing in mind what I've just been accused of and knowing how unstable he can be he says ' Bill can you do me a favour and change my wheel for me, but make sure you bring a blade incase I turn on you as I just don't know how these tablets will make me react when I see you?' What the fuck do you say to that?
I don't think many people would have gone over there but I did. I knew I hadn't done anything wrong but there was no way I was going to take a blade with me, not my style. He was my mate and I would have deal with it. Don't get me wrong, even though Roy is in his 70s, if he lands one on you, your gonna know about it so I didn't underestimate him at all but I also needed to go and see this through as I knew he wasn't responsible for his actions. A bit like the drunken uncle at a family party. You don't want to harm them in any way and just need to diffuse the situation in the best way you can. So I went over there and sorted his motor but I've got to be honest with you, the adrenaline was pumping away like fuck and if you can imagine being in the jungle and suddenly feeling a Silverback Gorilla of fucking Lion breathing on the back of your neck, and you freeze, hoping that it gives you a

miss, it felt like that. Since then we have been fine so maybe he doesn't mix his meds and booze. So that's a situation where a mate turned on me but I gave it a second chance because I understood there was other factors involved.

What did you do after you decided that you had outgrown living in a toilet?

I decided to have a break from doing robberies. I met this girl called Susan and went to live in Walton on the Naze and got back into boxing. Running along the sand and getting right back in the game. Moved on to a different girl and can't even remember her name. There was a ginger kid I became friends with, Michael Biles, a big lad who wanted to box, so I used to work out with him and show him some stuff. Bits of padwork etc. He picked it up fast, he was a natural. He ended up renting a room in the same place as me because his parents couldn't control him. This guest house was run by a lovely couple, Barry and Jean Evans, a Welsh couple. In one of the other rooms there was this guy about mid 30s who came back drunk one night and started banging on my door mouthing off. I was only about 17 at the time. So the door fly's open from the inside and I drag him in and batter fuck out of him. Just me in be boxers, what the fuck must it have looked like (laughs). Michael hears all the commotion and steams in like the fucking bells gone off for the next round. The drunken cunt is still mouthing off so we dragged him down the staircase and out into the street where Michael finished him off. If you added our ages up it came out to about the same age as the drunk so that seemed fair to me. That's the last we heard of him.

Later on in the same area I was working at Kilos leisure centre in Clacton and the Chippendales male strip act were touring and we wanted to get then in the centre for a drink to try and pull in some females. After that I was on the move again in-between Clacton, Cambridge, London. All this time I was driving about illegally and Churchill were always good for getting cover notes. They couldn't check DVLA databases like they do now, you could pay a deposit then and get the printed insurance through the post and then cancel it but keep the year's insurance certificate and drive about on that. I even used the Green Flag breakdown insurance they provided. That's really taking the piss. The funny thing is that now I'm legal and pay my insurance and breakdown, they wanna fucking interrogate you to provide you with the service you pay for. Remember that day we went out to Cambridge and you bought that sports car but we broke down cause the water pump died. Those cunts at the AA wouldn't come out to us because neither of us was pregnant. Fucking wankers.

You mentioned that you and Neil used to rob drug dealers, what was that all about?

I finished with nicking motors and twinning them up I went into robbing the drug dealers. The way I see it is that it's wrong to go and rob normal innocent hard working people but drug dealers don't fit into that category. They were earning bundles of money ruining people's lives like your sister so I would fucking go round there and ruin their week and charge them a lot of money for that privilege. I'm not cheap on house calls (laughs). We would go in balaclava and gloved up and talk in different accents. It was funny because sometimes in the heat of the moment we would boot the door in as a Paddy and a German and by the time we left we were talking Scottish and Asian, fucking funny that was! I was about 14 stone of solid mass at the time due to training hard. I was training at the Ford Galaxy with Dean McTurnan and big black Owen. So yeah I was well into robbing drug dealers. The ones in Tiptree, Harold Hill, and then areas were easy. One fucking place we done has a dirty fucking house and they had these two dogs who were living in squalor. Dogs had to dig through their own shit for food. So we tied the dealer up, pillow case over the head, Gaffa taped them to a chairs and robbed them of their money and dogs. They were Dobermans and we took them to a better place to

179

live rather than a fucking drug den. Drug dealers are my biggest pet hate, fucking detest them, they just ruin people's lives. It seems like every fucker is on drugs these days and if I blew out every mate that didn't take drugs then I would have no fucker to talk to, apart from you. I would have no problem killing a drug dealer.

So are you saying you have killed people?

Not at all. And I won't bullshit that I have because things like that are traceable and that's why when people lie about killing people, they make the story uncheckable. No I haven't killed anyone. I grew up with the scariest man alive, that's why I don't give a fuck about these wankers and showboaters with their plastic guns and fabricated pasts about killings and violence. It's all bullshit and they know it. Everyone knows it. They are fucking mugs. But I did actually get pulled in and questioned on a murder that took place but it was fuck all to do with me. I think that was in 96 when I was in Pentonville prison. This scew came into my cell and said PC1854, there are two coppers here to speak to you. I was intrigued to hear what they had to say because I've been up to so much shit I never know what's gonna surface. I met them and said nothing, just listened. They were talking shit and I didn't know anything about what they were saying. We were wasting each other time so that was the end of it until three days later they came and took me to Plumstead Police station for formal questioning. I just gave a 'no comment' all the way through the interview and that was the end of it. I wasn't giving them any opportunity to fit me up. Then there was the second murder that also had fuck all to do with me. That was about seven years later in 2003. I had history of running about with guns so that's why I got connected to it. That came to nothing though. That was around the time I decided that petrol should be free and I used to fill up me motor and tear out of petrol stations without paying. I was quite a good artist and would use eye liner that the women use to change the lettering on my number plate and once I had done the runner, simply wipe it off. But one time this fucking two foot high have a go hero fucking tried to stop me driving out. I had done this petrol station two times before and he must have recognised me by my eyeliner (laughs), so as I've filled up and got back in my motor, he has jumped in front of the car like kids do when they are playing Bulldog. I thought, what the fuck is he doing. He was actually going to try stop me driving out. Now I'm no Carol Vorderman, but my maths are good enough to work out that a car weighing a Tonne and half has no worries faced with a four stone jobsworth. I gave it plenty of revs and the cunt still didn't move so I drove through him. This guy would win a game of chicken any day. The fucker didn't move so I hit him and he bounced all over the motor like a pebble skimming across the water. He snapped my fucking brand new Ariel in the process and ended up laying on the floor like a starfish as I tore out. He was OK though as I had someone check it out.

What about the real estate business you were running?

(laughs) Yeah that was a right touch at the time but it was like playing Monopoly, I didn't own fuck all. It was just after I finished working with Tito the black guy with the dreadlocks. We did some good business together but he went into selling drugs so I moved on, didn't want any of that, no matter how much you could earn.
The property scam was bringing me in about ten grand a time. I would rent a flat somewhere then sub-let it. It was a grand deposit fot the new tenant but the rent was dirt cheap. So I had no shortage of calls for people wanting it. They would get their deposit back when they left so they were getting a right result. The only problem was that they didn't know that I had sub let it to nine other people who were all moving in on the same day. So I took ten lots of deposits and gave them a key to the flat. That was it, I was never to be seen again after that and had £10,000 in my pocket and all they had was a souvenir keyring. I did that scam time and time

again and had bundles of money. Once it was all over I would go and lay a deposit on another flat and do it all again, sometimes making £15,000. I did this all over the place except for London because that was just too close to home. Me and Tina were living it up at Lakeside and Bluewater and had a great time spending and going out. Reece was still a toddled then and the grandparents looked after him till he was about two or three until Tina got a nice place to settle and call her own. We didn't want to put Reece at any risk because I was still wanted by the old bill and also all the people I had ripped off. We knew he was safe and that was good enough for me. I couldn't move in with her properly because the old bill were raiding her place, me dads etc to find me, so I stayed with Black Neil in Walthamstow.

We got hold of a couple of moody licences and decided to have a go at lorry driving because there was always a scam on the lorries. Also there were no photo-cards then so it was easy to be someone else. We both got a job at this newspaper delivery place but I hadn't driven a lorry before but though it would be handy to learn so I could start nicking them. It was my very first night and I had to go out route learning and they sent me out with this prick who had little man syndrome. A mouthy horrible cunt.

He thinks he is my boss and I think he is a fucking plum, so we were never gonna get on. So were out and I'm doing all the donkey work while he is doing the driving and its fucking winding me up but I just gritted my teeth as I had a different agenda once I had learnt about the lorry game. Once all the heavy works done and he has finished treating me like a fucking paperboy and were almost finished, he get me to take over the driving so I can fucking chauffeur him home, the cunt. So OK if that's the way he wants it I will. I just wanted to get back and get away from the cunt before I lost it and bashed him up. So I'm in the driver's seat now and I haven't a fucking clue what I'm doing. He thinks I'm pissing about to scare him so he will drive but I'm about to turn the motorway into a fucking white knuckle ride. The roads were clear so no one else was at risk. I'm fucking driving this thing to the best *of my ability about 50mph when I misjudge my distance as I'm trying to overtake a lorry and take the front off our cab by driving into the back of this 18 wheeler articulated lorry. The little cunt with me got a better view as he has hit the window screen full force and left a fucking spider web imprint on the glass like a forehead print (laughs). This prick is laying on the floor bleeding and crying that his head is hanging off as the driver of the lorry I've hit is now out his motor. I've had to make it convincing and told him the guy with me had had a fit and grabbed the steering wheel and we need an ambulance urgently etc. So he is making his phone calls and I've done a Houdini and had it on me toes. I've never run as fast as that without being chased by the police. I ended up getting a cab back to Neil's and that obviously was the end of that job.*

When was your first escape from the police?

I got caught in this little Mini I had, the police followed me to Warren road in Chingford. They plotted up and nicked me and put me in a 5 door Golf unmarked old bill car. They had me in the back seat and there was an A4 pic of me in the front, so they was well after me. They cuffed me but one of the cuffs was a bit loose. I made out to sniff and wipe me nose and craftily dribbled on the cuff to give it a bit of lubrication. Even if I had to break the bones in my hand in the process, I was gonna get those cuffs off. They were more interested in getting me to Barkinside police station so they could go watch football that night. They must be so used to people getting in that car and just giving up. But I don't give up until there are no options left. At this time I still had options, or a plan but it would take some timing to work. It pretty dark by now so they couldn't see I had a cuff off by now. They were having a good old laugh trying to intimidate me and piss me off as they jollied each other up for capturing me. I new that if I tapped the inner door handle then the interior light would come on which meant the child lock wasn't on. So I've tapped it down in an accidental fashion ant the lights come on. This flash cunt copper goes 'Oh dear we don't want you falling out the door and hurting yourself', which was his way of saying if we want to, we can throw you out the car and you will 'accidently' get seriously hurt. All that tough talk didn't bother me as I knew I could have it on me toes if I got my timing right. My que was the brake lights of the car in front. As soon as they came on that was my trigger to get the fuck out that car and run like fuck, and that's exactly what I did. Right on target the front car had braked and our car has done the same and I'm out the cunting car. Plod grabs my jacket and just looks gutted as I slip out of it and I'm off. The fucking muppets must have felt right cunts. (laughs). They were too fucking lazy to chase me and knew they weren't gonna catch me. I've now changed from Billy Martindale into Red Rum and I'm over every fucking fence and shit that's in my way. I was strangled by a clothes line, fell in a pond, got covered in shit, stung and cut to bits by nettles and all sorts of crap. I've gone from looking Draper to more like something out of a Swamp Thing movie. . Next thing I know the helicopter is hovering over looking for me. I knew that if they caught me I was gonna get a kicking. Fuck that. So I found a shed and hid in a bundle of old rags and pulled this tarpaulin over me. I didn't want the heat sensor of the Helicopter picking out my body heat so this was the only thing I could come up with. I'd seen roadwork vans with tarmac steaming on the back of the flat backs when they do road maintenance and they always have a tarpaulin over it to keep the heat in. It wasn't a foolproof plan, but it's all I had because I couldn't outrun a helicopter. I don't know how long I was there but once the police sirens had stopped and the copter fucked off, I felt relieved. Well I say relieved but that's an understatement. I don't know how to explain it but I came out of the shed and looked up at the sky at the stars and it was just so peaceful. It was like a spiritual moment when my whole life just flashed by me and I thought to myself. What the fuck am I doing with my life? I was being hunted down like a pack of dogs after a fox, I'm covered in shit, cut, battered and bruised from everything that caught me on the great escape and for what? There was no family or friends around me. I was all alone and had this tiny moment to think about my life.

So you changed your life from that point?

Not because I've still got the handcuffs on and I'm still wanted and needed to get home or to a safe house. I think it was probably just one of those moments like when we get bad news and we make all these promises to ourselves that we will never do certain things again if everything could be put right, but it never lasts long does it. Or I might have just been just lightheaded from my Olympic run. But it was a moment I won't forget. Anyway after that I made my way to a set of garages and there was a car there with this couple and kid in the back. The fells had just got out and clocked me. It's one of those moments that can go right or wrong. Bearing in mind I looked like shit. This fella was switched on and clocked my hand wrapped up where I was hiding the cuffs. 'Can you help me mate, I've just been involved in something and need to get out the area a bit lively'. He said 'So that's what the old bill were all about, they were looking for you was they?', So I replied 'Are you Safe mate?'.

He knew the score; he was sound, 100%. I showed him the cuffs so he knew I wasn't a nutter that was not gonna rob him or cause harm to them. He laughed and said 'You escaped nice one, quick get in the motor'. He took me to his flat, sorted out a set of clothes and let me get cleaned up. He called a mate who came round with a junior hacksaw and they cut through these holding handcuffs like a hot knife through butter. They then hid me in the boot of this white Granada Scorpio and got me out the area. I owe them so much and if he ever reads this, you know who you are and please contact me so I can thank you. I had the coppers name chalked on the cuffs still so a day or so later I phoned the police station and made out I was gonna hand myself in (laughs) but only if I could speak to the copper that grabbed my jacket as I did my bunk. So they have put me through to

*him and I've said 'How do you feel now you cunt, you
fucking idiot, I bet all your mates are laughing at you now'
and just laughed at him. 'enjoy your football match that night
you mug', and I'm just laughing at him as he is threatening
and cunting me off. I just can't help myself at times and just
had to do it, which made the cat and mouse chase even worse
for me. They were only doing their job and me mine so it
wasn't really personal. Even to this day I don't hate the
police but I would still never do any sort of deal with them,
But we need the old bill to keep society in order. They are
just doing a job.*

Didn't you escape again from the police?

*Yeah, it was when some cunt grassed me up. I was staying
with my mate Rob Joseph in Harcourt Avenue, Manor Park.
So the house phone rings and I answer but no one speaks. At
this time my ex Kelly is still on a mission to have me nicked.
She is pissed off because I went off with her cousin Tina, who
I've been with ever since, so she is a woman scorned who
wants revenge and had informed the old bill of everything
that I had ever done, the bast'd. A right fucking nasty bunny
boiler. Anyway about half hour later there's a knock at the
door. Now Robs flat was the top half of this old Victorian
house with a steep staircase to climb to get to the flat. But
first you have to come through the main door that faces the
street. I've looked out the window and saw two CID I
recognised, Mr & Mrs Bernie McCabe and a right pair of
wrong-uns I found out later on. So I've had it out the back
window, standing on the window sill when I hear a voice 'Oy
stay where you are' and I've looked down and there's four
big lumps, old bill waiting for me. 'fuck off you cunts' and
I've jumped sideways into the next garden. I'm quite agile as
I was 13 half stone then so I'm across next doors porch and
over the next garden. I've done about 20 gardens and I'm
fucked so kick the back door in only to find this woman who's
just got out the bath and just wrapped in a towel. Next thing
the old bill have sussed where I am and try to force the back
door open as I'm holding it shut. I've picked my moment and*

let the door fly as I've run to the front door, pulling stuff over behind me. The fuckers locked so there was no way out. In desperation I've taken the only option left and that's to throw myself through the Victorian sash window and still have the scar as a reminder on the top of my left arm and my hand. When they finally caught me, they described it in court as me going through the window in SAS style (laughs), that's exactly what they said. So I'm running down the road with the net curtains still wrapped round me like a fucking Sari. Then this old bill car pulls in front of me and this little bird gets out who was a dead ringer for that little scary woman with the weird voice in Poltergeist. 'Come here, stay where you are'. Er, I don't think so, and I'm off. The only place I could find to hide was this big wheel bin full of slops. I was heaving but had no choice. After about an hour I climbed out and knocked on a door which this woman answers. 'Any chance you can call me a cab', and she laughs 'they looking for you', and invites me in. That's the good thing about the East End, people look after each other like that. So she has called me a cab and gives me a jumper to put on, and this little blue umbrella. How freaky is this, the handle of it was a wooden carving of a London Bobby, a copper (laughs). So I've thanked her and got the cab to Leytonstone. Got myself some cloned credit cards and I'm back out working the shop like nothing has happened. The cards were good for buying booze and fags and as I didn't smoke or drink then, I would sell it all and that paid my wages until I got back on my feet. There was another time I got nicked and was caught with wheels off a car that I stole and I was wanted still at that time. Me and Garvey got done and taken into Romford nick. We had moody names and I gave Jason Miller. They printed me and let me out on bail without even realizing who I was. They fucked right up there (laughs). Oh and another time when I was going under the name of William Green, coz I had a moody passport in that name, I was working at this car sales place but they were getting greedy and tried to cut my money once I had created sales. So I left. But on the day I left some punter went in and paid £7,000 cash for a car that

187

allegedly went missing. I was the obvious culprit or easy person to blame but it wasn't down to me. So somebody wanted the money back and I find that I'm being followed so it's developed into a chase. I was wanted so didn't want to bring attention to myself but this cunt is right on my case and the car chase is through the streets of Dagenham. I've rammed the cunt to warn him off but he is still on me and then this fucking cabbie involves himself in the chase and blocks my exit, so I ram that cunt as well. I'm clean away and drive smack into an old bill car. They drag me out and I'm back down Romford nick and bailed out again as William Green.

You told me once about an incident you had with a Volvo, can you repeat that for the book?

I had this right old shitter of a Volvo, but I was pretty skint at the time so it was better than walking. Anyway I'm doing some bits of work and I'm asked to collect a debt and I would get £150 for my time. So I went round to this guys house and tells him I'm here to collect. But he's talking to me out the top window and won't come down. 'Tell your mate to go fuck himself, I'm not paying'. So I make the call an pass on the message and get told I'm not getting paid if I don't collect. So that's it, I want this fella to come to the door so I can persuade him to pay. 'Come down and speak to me, I'm sure we can sort this out', but next thing I know he has thrown a cup of warm piss all over me. The dirty cunt. So that it, I've got in the motor and reversed it up the drive as this cunt is laughing at me. I'm out of control now. My foot has gone to the floor with the throttle and I've driven the Volvo right through the front of his house. The car is now in his living room and I'm stuck in the motor where his TV and video has jammed the door. All I can think about now is the old bill coming so I've reversed back out with a lot of effort, spun it round and fucked off. The car was scrapped and I got knocked for my money. But at least I didn't get nicked. I've got a brilliant track record in as much that there isn't many

188

villainous crimes that I haven't committed yet I've never been convicted of anything. There nothing clever about doing bird or getting convicted for something but it takes a real clever fucker to commit crime for two decades and never get convicted for any of it. What can you do in prison? You can't rent out flats, rob places, steal cars, do credit card fraud. All you can do is put up with the smell of other peoples shit and piss while the screws are giving you shit. So big fucking deal if all someone can brag about is how much bird they have done. It's a waste of life. For the select few maybe prison does pay if they have earnt enough to warrant it but it's a bit like boxing. Only a handful made the real money while all the others take the same beatings and end up with fuck all.

The last thing you got nicked for was a major fraud on high value cars wasn't it?

Yeah, Crane and Mayo came and nicked me for a £30,000 fraud on a Ferrari that they said I had sold to a guy in Australia but I allegedly smashed up and sent to him in pieces (laughs). They wanted to take it to Crown Court at a cost of £25,000 a day. All they had was a photo of me standing next to a red Ferrari that looked the same as the one that got sold, allegedly by me, and when they raided my house they took my computer and found a picture of a smashed up red Ferrari but they couldn't number plate it because that must have got lost in the crash (laughs). This bollocks went on for a year and then got a 'no further action'. That was a result to get off with something that they alleged I did.

So did you go out and celebrate?
(laughs) Yeah by getting nicked again that night. There was a mini festival thing going on in Ongar so I took my boy Lewis to the fair. He was about nine then. Anyway the first thing he wants to do is go on the air rifles and try win a prize for his mum, so I gave him a couple of quid and over he goes. As he is trying to pay his money the guy behind the counter says

189

'fucking wait ur turn, I tell you when you can have a turn'. I've heard this so I'm off and having words with this fucking mongrel cunt. No one speaks to my boy like that; he's nine years old for fuck sake. So this prick thinks he is bit of a chap and fucking mumbles something about being fucked off with all these kids? The cunt is working a fucking stall in a community festival. What the fuck is he doing there? So I've grabbed the air rifle and stuck the end of it in his eye line. 'you fucking want some of this you arrogant cunt'. He is now clucking like a chicken and full of fucking apologies. The wanker. I walked off and left it at that. Next thing I know these to Police Specials come and have a work with me about grabbing this guy etc, which I didn't. So I've told them to fuck off and then the old bill arrive and I'm 'invited' into Ongar nick where they arrest me. Cunts! I went there of my own accord to explain myself and the dirty cunts arrest me. They were too scared to cuff me so called in Loughton old bill who came down and took me away. They knew it was all bollocks so eventually let me go. The funny thing was that this fat cunt wannabe copper on the desk leaves the witness statement on show so I've clocked the scumbags name and address. I went and thanked him at a later date in my own special way. Allegedly! (laughs).

What's the funniest thing you can remember related to work?

(Laughing) I was working for a private investigator, a good pal and he would give me the stuff that he wasn't really interested in. So a job came in for a woman who thinks her old man is cheating on her and wants him followed in the Hackney area. Piss easy job because the man has practically no eyesight and is only a hairline away from being 100% blind. This guy is a DJ but obviously cannot drive cause he can't see fuck all. So I've got triple X Paul to help me on this one as the guy would leave his home and get in a cab, which Paul would follow in his motor or I would follow him on foot if he walks as the car was not able to go that way. So were *plotted up and hiding, habit I suppose because he couldn't see us if we were right in front of him. He came out the house and decides to walk so I'm on the case. Paul stays with the car. I've followed him a few yards up the road and he stands by this bus stop where I assume he is waiting for someone to arrive. The bus arrives and he fucking gets on it, I didn't expect that and had no money on me. I've run back to Paul to grab a couple of quid but the bus had gone. We fucking lost him. How fucking embarrassing is that, losing a blind man that you're following (laughs).*

What was the recent incident you had at the Sugar Hut in Brentwood?

It wasn't the Sugar Hut, we had just left there and the Litten Tree and decided to end up at Sams. There's me and Tina, Roy Shaw, triple X Paul, Rob and his brother etc. Just a group of people out having a laugh. We get to Sams and this fat cunt bouncer who looked like that poof Russell Grant refuses us entry. Word had reached them that Roy Shaw and Billy Martindale were in town so keep an eye on them. I admit we do get a bit out of hand at times but this night we were having a nice evening. We should have stayed in the Sugar Hut as it was lovely in there. So were at Sams and there is this wall of doormen that look more like bin men and were get refused entry. So the Russell Grant lookalikee and his side kick, this skinny twig with his Hi-vis jacket and wooly hat try and earn their colours in front of their fellow bouncers. 'You're not coming in, there seven of you, our policy doesn't allow groups of seven or more' So I'm pissed off 'There's six of us you stupid cunt, come here and I will bite your fucking nose off'. Jay'm you know yourself from working the doors that once you say NO, it's NO and you have to deal with that whichever way it goes. So they have called the manager out. What wankers, they were employed to deal with people at the door, not the manager. So this Alan Carr clone comes out and introduces himself as the manager. I've said 'You look like Alan Carr you cunt and if you don't

*let us in we are gonna tear through your door staff and come
in anyway, what way do you want it?'. Roy was actually
being diplomatic about the whole thing but I'm not being
cunted off like that. In the meantime this fucking Bosnian
wannabe doorman runs out to deal with us, thinking it was a
bunch of kids trying to get in. You get these sort is silly cunts
at all the clubs, wannabee doormen who try befriending
doorstaff by dealing with minor problems for them. So this
guy comes tearing through the doors with his chest puffed out
and saw us lot ' Fuck of back inside Bosnian Bob before you
get some' I shouted, he then u-turns back in the club. The
manager is in a no win situation now so backs down and lets
us in. What a cunt. He tells the doorstaff to refuse us entry
and then he lets us in. He has now well undermined them and
they feel fucking stupid. The head doorman should have said
to the manager 'you can fuck off, we have told them there not
in and that stands'. What the manager did to them was wrong
but we were in so that was it. When we got in we got the VIP
area etc and had a good night. Even Bosnian Bob came over
with a bottle of Champagne, and turned out to be OK, and
Spanish or something, but not Bosnian. We proved to
everyone that we were just out to have a nice evening and
that's all we did. When we left we thanked them and help no
malice towards any of them.*

You told me once you was glad to go into Pentonville, why?

*Prior to that I spent five days in a police cell on me own just
going from court to court, Bow, Barking etc. It was driving
me made being on my own. You know what I'm like, I have to
be busying myself with things and chatting to people. I can't
stand being alone. So I knew that after five days I wasn't
getting bail so I just wanted to get to prison and be with
others. When I got there I overheard that Billy Williams
'Jango' was there so at least there was someone I knew I
could chat with. When I was being processed I had to see the
doctor and I told him I felt suicidal, I didn't, I just wanted to*

up. They were in the Bear in Harold hill. I speak to
on the mobile and they are laughing at me. That's it,
aving none of that so I've flown down to the Bear and
ed fuck out of them. I seriously served them up and left
with busted ribs, missing teeth broken bones, busted
tc. When I go into one, I go, and these two cunts took
a mug. That's the bit that happened and I did it on my
nd smashed the pair of them to pieces. The next bit is
they alleged happened when they became police
rs; well that's what grasses are isn't it? They said
er they still wasn't able to pay me my money, I went
o their workshop with a shotgun and blew a hole in it
em on the other side. I then allegedly tried to shoot
d demanded my money. The rest you already know.
bill came round firm handed and armed and nicked
t. I won't go into it because it's covered in the book.
would I need a shotgun to shoot a hole in their door
threaten them, when I've already smashed the pair
with my bare hands and got nothing other than
on. They sold my five cars and had a nice few grand
while I got fuckall. I just look at it as Karma for all
e I've ripped off. I learnt from that experience and
de that mistake again, an expensive lesson.

----

ow you have lots more to tell but we are at the
r time so need to finish here. I'm sure people
forward to you doing talks and book signings
can tell the other encounters not in the book.
u for your time. The last few months of me
working with you on this book, has been
g, to say the least. We wish you all the best
ou go forward feeding the right Wolf!
t

be put on a wing with a TV. So Doc said 'OK then we will put
you in a padded cell, take your laces, belt and everything you
might harm yourself with and will stick you in a jacket to stop
you self harming'. He knew I was at it 'You know what Doc, I
feel better already' and I laughed, so did he. So he didn't
Fraggle me off (laughs).

How was it in there?
The first fella they put me in with is this weird fat fella from
Basildon who was sitting there shaving his legs. Fuck that!
But he was out in a week so I didn't have to worry about him
too much. The worst thing about being on remand though is
that you just don't know how long your gonna be there. At
least if I had a two stretch or five etc I would adjust better
because I would be able to pace myself but when you just
don't know its fucking horrible. Especially when you don't
even know what your charges are or what they will find on
you whilst you're inside. After shavy legs man I was banged
up with Patrick Gallagher, a good boxer who was involved
with Frank Warren's camp. He was a nice guy. We kicked off
with two cons in there over something and I used my belt and
done the business with the buckle and he used a tin of Tuna
and we cut these to mugs up.
So we then get split up and I'm moved to G-Wing. Got a pool
table, TV with stuff like the Trisha Show which I was on
recently, but I think it was on a different channel then. The
food is shit, nothing tastes like it should but you get used to
it. You could have a radio but not Duracell batteries because
they could be used to make bombs so it was just the shit
cheap batteries that didn't last long. We would have to hold
them under a hot tap to give them a bit more life and could
use them a bit longer. Once you were locked up in your cell
there was fuck all to do. We had a Monopoly game that we
would share and had it for a night each. That was about as
exciting as the nights go. Money was tight so people found
ways to make the best of what they had. One guy would get a
razor and split a single match into four and get a load of
toilet roll and screw it up really tight, light it and blow it out.

It would then smoulder all night and was good enough to light cigarettes. I didn't smoke them so I would buy tobacco and trade it for phone cards. I think the limit was about £12 a week we were allowed to spend on phone cards but I wanted more.

August 8th 2006 I was released on Judge and Chambers bail which is very hard to get, so I was lucky.

You said you were involved in a bit of doorwork, when did that begin?

Well I did a few different places in Essex and London. But I wasn't into it full on like you, Micky Bennett and my dad; I was just making ends meet till the next scam came along. My first night on the door was at the Litten Tree in Old Street in 2000 I think for Reg who owned Raven Security. I was dressed like a cunt in my dogtooth jacket and Litten Tree green tie, white shirt and black trousers. People don't look at you the same way as they do with proper security clothing on. Anyway I'm dressed like this and I end up working the night on my own and it football night, there was some footy thing going on at the time but I don't follow football so couldn't tell you what it was. I also worked there with big black Selwin, a lovely fella and former bodybuilder and your pal Teddy boy Mick, Micky Bennet. I know he's not a Teddyboy but he has a Rock n Roll haircut and tattoos so that's the best way I can describe him. I wanted to go and see him in hospital recently when he had his heart bypass but you wouldn't tell me where he was you git. There wasn't much trouble there apart from the Friday night Hooray Henrys but it did go off one time with this mob of Eastern Europeans. They were coming back to smash the place up so Reg arranged for a load of bikers to come down to help out. Think they might have been Hells Angels or something like that. They were the real thing and not a group to fuck with. But the Eastern European lot got wind of it and didn't show. I did some other places like the Cauliflower in Ilford, the Army and Navy with Mick, TJays in Silvertown – the only white person in a Nigerian club, Chadwell Arms in Chadwell

Heath, I did the Conneaut rooms and pulle[d] for the Sheik event, and just kept moving fr[om] because I didn't have a badge. I cou[ld] registered door supervisor because I was s[till on the] run and didn't even have a driving licence. [Up] to 2003 I kind of slowed down and got mo[re] so that really was it for the doorwork.

Bill some people say that you can't kee[p] what's that all about?

I don't know. I piss people off or they p[eople] just seem to escalate to a point that ca[n] that say Billy can't keep a friend or B[illy] can say is they obviously have their rea[son] be saying it. But I had a pal called Ia[n] a Scottish born Yorkshire accent nor[thern] was Yugoslavian and he has been my [friend to this] day. So maybe it's just the wannab[e] don't stay friends with me because[e] bullshit. I don't give a fuck about fake[e] mates like Ian and his dad that are [real and] accept you for what you are and [when I] worked with them in their building c[ompany]

You have ripped a lot of people [that were close] to you?

Yeah, there were these to cunts in [Essex] and Will Bainbridge. They were [my age] maybe older and were bit of an [...] area but not in the bigger circle [...] of smashing someone up in a [...] someone in a pub. Just bully bo[ys ...] motors off me and they were g[...] when they sold then. Time pass[ed ...] gone but I hadn't seen any c[...] chasing them up and getting [...]

them
them
I'm [...]
smas[...]
them [...]
jaws [...]
me fo[r ...]
own a[...]
what [...]
inform[...]
that af[...]
round [...]
with th[...]
them a[...]
The old[...]
me for [...]
But why[...]
and ther[...]
of them [...]
satisfact[...]
out of it [...]
the peop[...]
never ma[...]

Bill, I kn[ow ...]
end of ou[r ...]
will look[...]
where yo[u ...]
Thank yo[u ...]
and Paul [...]
challengin[g ...]
and hope [...]
All the bes[t ...]

Jamie

Other books to look out for

Danny's first book 'We Dared' sold out completely and has now become a collector's item. Don't miss the opportunity to get a copy of his new book 'Wild Cats. A Hard-hitting account of notorious East End gangster, Danny Woollard, who was arrested in 1995 for his involvement in a multimillion pound robbery on a security van. Written in his own words by the man himself. See Danny in the new film 'The End'.

Available from New Breed Publishing – mail order
www.newbreedbooks.co.uk
New Breed
Po box 2676
Romford
Essex
RM7 0WA

A cut above the rest
The Cliff Field story
By
Paul Knight & Jamie O'Keefe
Due out Feb 2009

Available from New Breed Publishing – mail order
<u>*www.newbreedbooks.co.uk*</u>

New Breed
Po box 2676
Romford
Essex
RM7 0WA

THUGS MUGS & VIOLENCE

By
Jamie O'Keefe

Available from New Breed Publishing – mail order
www.newbreedbooks.co.uk

New Breed
Po box 2676
Romford
Essex
RM7 0WA

No One Fears when Angry

Jamie O'Keefe

Jamie O'Keefe has spent years studying, training and teaching the Fighting Arts. He presently holds the rank of 7th Dan black belt with the 'The Self Defence Federation' and is the chief instructor of his own 'New Breed system of Self Protection.' Additionally he is also a former bouncer and has spent 15-years working the door. Whilst working as a doorman Jamie studied and gained his City & Guilds *'Further and adult education*

teachers certificate' and then his Cert ed. *'Certificate in Education and training'* from Greenwich University. He is also an NVQ Assessor and *'Founder fellow of the Society of Martial Arts, (F.S.M.A.)* Jamie has written many articles for Martial Arts magazines and is a former columnist for 'Martial arts illustrated and regular columnists with Combat magazine.' He has also been featured in 'Later' and 'Front' magazines. He has also appeared on BBC radio and on Television as an authority on Self-protection. Plus he also features in the ITV seven week series 'Bouncers'. Jamie was inducted into the Martial Arts Hall of Fame three times for his 25 years dedication and promotion of the Martial Arts worldwide.

He has spent the best part of his life in contact with people displaying anger in some shape or form and has now put pen to paper in the hope that he can put his own, and many other people's anger to rest.

Available from New Breed Publishing – mail order

New Breed
Po box 2676
Romford
Essex
RM7 0WA

Since entering secondary school, the Author **Jamie O'Keefe** has been exposed to the supposed school playground 'Tough guys' commonly known as bullies. Realising that he needed to learn to protect himself he went on to spend over 25 years within the martial arts initially for self-defence which later progressed to teaching self-protection. Throughout his travels he had much exposure of street fighting from both the position of the victim then later on as an exponent of self-protection.

He also spent half his life as a doorman dealing with the violence within Pub's, Clubs, and live music venues within the heart of London's night-life. Throughout his time as both a self-protection instructor and Doorman, he has seen literally thousands of situations where individuals act-like tough guys, or pose themselves as tough guys. Whilst training to become a teacher with Greenwich University, his studies introduced him to the problem solving and line of questioning of the Greek Philosophers, namely Plato. This led him to think more in-depth about a question that he knew many people had been pondering over for years. 'What makes Tough guys Tough?' As a result he decided to put this question to self-protection instructors, Bouncers, Boxers, Bodyguards, Soldiers, T.A.s, Streetfighters and more. Within this book you will find the most revealing answers on the subject of what makes tough guys tough, along with the secret combination of attributing factors that will make you tougher than you are now.

This is the only book in print of its kind that digs deep into the secret domain the undiscovered area, of 'What makes Tough guys Tough!'

www.newbreedbooks.co.uk

New Breed, Po box 2676, Romford, Essex, RM7 0WA

Coding of a Concrete Animal
by Paul Knight

This book chronicles the extraordinary life, exploits and adventures of Billy Michaels. Born into a family steeped in nefarious deeds and activity, Billy's fate was cast from the cradle, questioning whether it's genetics that provides a life pattern, or just fate. Billy learns the hard way that by fulfilling his bloodline's destiny, a life of crime and violence can get you where you want to be. Proving the fact that brain can beat brawn, schoolboy Billy falls in as a leader of the local gang, moving from demanding treats with menace from local vendors to running the neighbourhood drug trade. Billy, learning the tricks of his predestined trade from masters in the field, proves to be quite adept and effective in this endeavour. As his firm work their way up the criminal food chain, their futures appear to be nothing more than a litany of successful and profitable capers, events as they would have anticipated weren't exactly as they expected. After the overdose of one of his closest friends, Billy embarks on a drunken path of violent redemption, which leads him to the dark world of vice and security. By the time the end comes to his teenage years, Billy has witnessed death, experienced loss, repaid emotional debts and found the true meaning of sacrifice. This is the story of Billy Michaels, his East End heritage and his love for his brothers and extended family. A family that becomes at odds with choices made and sides taken within the criminal world that serves to destroy the oaths and family ties made by love and blood. As all their unflinching attitudes to life and the acceptance of 'normality' which those on the outside may think immoral and destructive become common practice. This is the Billy Michaels story, the animal from the concrete jungle.

Available from New Breed Publishing – mail order
www.newbreedbooks.co.uk

New Breed
Po box 2676
Romford
Essex
RM7 0WA

Old School - New School

A guide to Bouncers - Security and Registered Door Supervisors

Jamie O'Keefe has spent most of his adult life working within different areas of Security through the late 70s, 80s, and 90s. A majority of this time has been spent working the doors of Pub's, Clubs, and Live music venues within the heart of London's night-life. Although his role is now mainly within the education and training of security awareness within the leisure and retail industry. He has also spent much of  his time working within some of the seediest back street clubs within London's notorious East End and Soho, dealing with people from all walks of life. Jamie is also a 7th Dan Black belt and Self protection instructor and spent his last few years relaxing from his nights on the door, by writing his first book 'Dog's don't Know Kung fu - a guide to female Self Protection.' This focused on his many years as a Self Protection instructor plus his 28 year study and analysis of the martial arts. He then went on to research and write this book 'Old School-New School' which focuses on the changes and evolution of the Bouncers of old, to the modern day Door Supervisors. This book covers the areas of Criminal and Licensing law, drugs, first aid, self protection, fire safety, the councils training requirements, along with many of Jamie's own personal reflections and thoughts on Bouncers and the role of Door supervisor's. If security within the leisure industry affects you or the safety of the environment within which you work - no matter how remote, you should read this book. It's a Blueprint for the future of Security!

Available from New Breed Publishing – mail order www.newbreedbooks.co.uk

New Breed, Po box 2676, Romford, Essex, RM7 0WA

Wild Thing: The True Story of
Britain's Rightful Guv'nor (Paperback)

Lew Yates

Due out

8 Jan 2009

be put on a wing with a TV. So Doc said 'OK then we will put you in a padded cell, take your laces, belt and everything you might harm yourself with and will stick you in a jacket to stop you self harming'. He knew I was at it 'You know what Doc, I feel better already' and I laughed, so did he. So he didn't Fraggle me off (laughs).

How was it in there?

The first fella they put me in with is this weird fat fella from Basildon who was sitting there shaving his legs. Fuck that! But he was out in a week so I didn't have to worry about him too much. The worst thing about being on remand though is that you just don't know how long your gonna be there. At least if I had a two stretch or five etc I would adjust better because I would be able to pace myself but when you just don't know its fucking horrible. Especially when you don't even know what your charges are or what they will find on you whilst you're inside. After shavy legs man I was banged up with Patrick Gallagher, a good boxer who was involved with Frank Warren's camp. He was a nice guy. We kicked off with two cons in there over something and I used my belt and done the business with the buckle and he used a tin of Tuna and we cut these to mugs up.

So we then get split up and I'm moved to G-Wing. Got a pool table, TV with stuff like the Trisha Show which I was on recently, but I think it was on a different channel then. The food is shit, nothing tastes like it should but you get used to it. You could have a radio but not Duracell batteries because they could be used to make bombs so it was just the shit cheap batteries that didn't last long. We would have to hold them under a hot tap to give them a bit more life and could use them a bit longer. Once you were locked up in your cell there was fuck all to do. We had a Monopoly game that we would share and had it for a night each. That was about as exciting as the nights go. Money was tight so people found ways to make the best of what they had. One guy would get a razor and split a single match into four and get a load of toilet roll and screw it up really tight, light it and blow it out.

193

It would then smoulder all night and was good enough to light cigarettes. I didn't smoke them so I would buy tobacco and trade it for phone cards. I think the limit was about £12 a week we were allowed to spend on phone cards but I wanted more.

August 8th 2006 I was released on Judge and Chambers bail which is very hard to get, so I was lucky.

You said you were involved in a bit of doorwork, when did that begin?

Well I did a few different places in Essex and London. But I wasn't into it full on like you, Micky Bennett and my dad; I was just making ends meet till the next scam came along. My first night on the door was at the Litten Tree in Old Street in 2000 I think for Reg who owned Raven Security. I was dressed like a cunt in my dogtooth jacket and Litten Tree green tie, white shirt and black trousers. People don't look at you the same way as they do with proper security clothing on. Anyway I'm dressed like this and I end up working the night on my own and it football night, there was some footy thing going on at the time but I don't follow football so couldn't tell you what it was. I also worked there with big black Selwin, a lovely fella and former bodybuilder and your pal Teddy boy Mick, Micky Bennet. I know he's not a Teddyboy but he has a Rock n Roll haircut and tattoos so that's the best way I can describe him. I wanted to go and see him in hospital recently when he had his heart bypass but you wouldn't tell me where he was you git. There wasn't much trouble there apart from the Friday night Hooray Henrys but it did go off one time with this mob of Eastern Europeans. They were coming back to smash the place up so Reg arranged for a load of bikers to come down to help out. Think they might have been Hells Angels or something like that. They were the real thing and not a group to fuck with. But the Eastern European lot got wind of it and didn't show. I did some other places like the Cauliflower in Ilford, the Army and Navy with Mick, TJays in Silvertown – the only white person in a Nigerian club, Chadwell Arms in Chadwell

Heath, I did the Conneaut rooms and pulled in 30 doormen for the Sheik event, and just kept moving from place to place because I didn't have a badge. I couldn't become a registered door supervisor because I was still wanted on the run and didn't even have a driving licence. After that in 2002 to 2003 I kind of slowed down and got more into selling cars so that really was it for the doorwork.

Bill some people say that you can't keep a friend for long, what's that all about?

I don't know. I piss people off or they piss me off and things just seem to escalate to a point that can't be fixed. To those that say Billy can't keep a friend or Billy's a bastard, all I can say is they obviously have their reasons or they wouldn't be saying it. But I had a pal called Ian Rajasalyvic who was a Scottish born Yorkshire accent northern fella, who's dad was Yugoslavian and he has been my mate for years to this day. So maybe it's just the wannabee gangster types that don't stay friends with me because I can suss out their bullshit. I don't give a fuck about fake gangster wanksters. Its mates like Ian and his dad that are real mates. People that accept you for what you are and treat you with respect. I worked with them in their building company for about a year.

You have ripped a lot of people off, has it ever happened to you?

Yeah, there were these to cunts in Harold Hill, Steve Brown and Will Bainbridge. They were probably about my age, maybe older and were bit of an handful in the Harold Hill area but not in the bigger circles. They would think nothing of smashing someone up in a road rage or hammering someone in a pub. Just bully boys I suppose. They had a few motors off me and they were gonna sell them and pay me when they sold then. Time passed and I heard the motors had gone but I hadn't seen any cash. So after a few weeks of chasing them up and getting tired of the excuses I phoned *them up. They were in the Bear in Harold hill. I speak to them on the mobile and they are laughing at me. That's it, I'm having none of that so I've flown down to the Bear and smashed fuck out of them. I seriously served them up and left them with busted ribs, missing teeth broken bones, busted jaws etc. When I go into one, I go, and these two cunts took me for a mug. That's the bit that happened and I did it on my own and smashed the pair of them to pieces. The next bit is what they alleged happened when they became police informers; well that's what grasses are isn't it? They said that after they still wasn't able to pay me my money, I went round to their workshop with a shotgun and blew a hole in it with them on the other side. I then allegedly tried to shoot them and demanded my money. The rest you already know. The old bill came round firm handed and armed and nicked me for it. I won't go into it because it's covered in the book. But why would I need a shotgun to shoot a hole in their door and then threaten them, when I've already smashed the pair of them with my bare hands and got nothing other than satisfaction. They sold my five cars and had a nice few grand out of it while I got fuckall. I just look at it as Karma for all the people I've ripped off. I learnt from that experience and never made that mistake again, an expensive lesson.*

Bill, I know you have lots more to tell but we are at the end of our time so need to finish here. I'm sure people will look forward to you doing talks and book signings where you can tell the other encounters not in the book. Thank you for your time. The last few months of me and Paul working with you on this book, has been challenging, to say the least. We wish you all the best and hope you go forward feeding the right Wolf!

All the best

Jamie

Other books to look out for

Danny's first book 'We Dared' sold out completely and has now become a collector's item. Don't miss the opportunity to get a copy of his new book 'Wild Cats. A Hard-hitting account of notorious East End gangster, Danny Woollard, who was arrested in 1995 for his involvement in a multimillion pound robbery on a security van. Written in his own words by the man himself. See Danny in the new film 'The End'.

Available from New Breed Publishing – mail order
www.newbreedbooks.co.uk
New Breed
Po box 2676
Romford
Essex
RM7 0WA

A cut above the rest
The Cliff Field story
By
Paul Knight & Jamie O'Keefe
Due out Feb 2009

Available from New Breed Publishing – mail order
www.newbreedbooks.co.uk

New Breed
Po box 2676
Romford
Essex
RM7 0WA

THUGS MUGS & VIOLENCE

By
Jamie O'Keefe

Available from New Breed Publishing – mail order
www.newbreedbooks.co.uk
New Breed
Po box 2676
Romford
Essex
RM7 0WA

No One Fears when Angry

By
Jamie O'Keefe

Jamie O'Keefe has spent years studying, training and teaching the Fighting Arts. He presently holds the rank of 7th Dan black belt with the 'The Self Defence Federation' and is the chief instructor of his own 'New Breed system of Self Protection.' Additionally he is also a former bouncer and has spent 15-years working the door. Whilst working as a doorman Jamie studied and gained his City & Guilds *'Further and adult education*

teachers certificate' and then his Cert ed. *'Certificate in Education and training'* from Greenwich University. He is also an NVQ Assessor and *'Founder fellow of the Society of Martial Arts, (F.S.M.A.)* Jamie has written many articles for Martial Arts magazines and is a former columnist for 'Martial arts illustrated and regular columnists with Combat magazine.' He has also been featured in 'Later' and 'Front' magazines. He has also appeared on BBC radio and on Television as an authority on Self-protection. Plus he also features in the ITV seven week series 'Bouncers'. Jamie was inducted into the Martial Arts Hall of Fame three times for his 25 years dedication and promotion of the Martial Arts worldwide.

He has spent the best part of his life in contact with people displaying anger in some shape or form and has now put pen to paper in the hope that he can put his own, and many other people's anger to rest.

Available from New Breed Publishing – mail order
www.newbreedbooks.co.uk

New Breed
Po box 2676
Romford
Essex
RM7 0WA

Since entering secondary school, the Author **Jamie O'Keefe** has been exposed to the supposed school playground 'Tough guys' commonly known as bullies. Realising that he needed to learn to protect himself he went on to spend over 25 years within the martial arts initially for self-defence which later progressed to teaching self-protection. Throughout his travels he had much exposure of street fighting from both the position of the victim then later on as an exponent of self-protection.

He also spent half his life as a doorman dealing with the violence within Pub's, Clubs, and live music venues within the heart of London's night-life. Throughout his time as both a self-protection instructor and Doorman, he has seen literally thousands of situations where individuals act-like tough guys, or pose themselves as tough guys. Whilst training to become a teacher with Greenwich University, his studies introduced him to the problem solving and line of questioning of the Greek Philosophers, namely Plato. This led him to think more in-depth about a question that he knew many people had been pondering over for years. 'What makes Tough guys Tough?' As a result he decided to put this question to self-protection instructors, Bouncers, Boxers, Bodyguards, Soldiers, T.A.s, Streetfighters and more. Within this book you will find the most revealing answers on the subject of what makes tough guys tough, along with the secret combination of attributing factors that will make you tougher than you are now.

This is the only book in print of its kind that digs deep into the secret domain the undiscovered area, of 'What makes Tough guys Tough!'

www.newbreedbooks.co.uk

New Breed, Po box 2676, Romford, Essex, RM7 0WA

Coding of a Concrete Animal

by Paul Knight

This book chronicles the extraordinary life, exploits and adventures of Billy Michaels. Born into a family steeped in nefarious deeds and activity, Billy's fate was cast from the cradle, questioning whether it's genetics that provides a life pattern, or just fate. Billy learns the hard way that by fulfilling his bloodline's destiny, a life of crime and violence can get you where you want to be. Proving the fact that brain can beat brawn, schoolboy Billy falls in as a leader of the local gang, moving from demanding treats with menace from local vendors to running the neighbourhood drug trade. Billy, learning the tricks of his predestined trade from masters in the field, proves to be quite adept

and effective in this endeavour. As his firm work their way up the criminal food chain, their futures appear to be nothing more than a litany of successful and profitable capers, events as they would have anticipated weren't exactly as they expected. After the overdose of one of his closest friends, Billy embarks on a drunken path of violent redemption, which leads him to the dark world of vice and security. By the time the end comes to his teenage years, Billy has witnessed death, experienced loss, repaid emotional debts and found the true meaning of sacrifice. This is the story of Billy Michaels, his East End heritage and his love for his brothers and extended family. A family that becomes at odds with choices made and sides taken within the criminal world that serves to destroy the oaths and family ties made by love and blood. As all their unflinching attitudes to life and the acceptance of 'normality' which those on the outside may think immoral and destructive become common practice. This is the Billy Michaels story, the animal from the concrete jungle.

Available from New Breed Publishing – mail order
www.newbreedbooks.co.uk

New Breed
Po box 2676
Romford
Essex
RM7 0WA

Old School - New School

A guide to Bouncers - Security and Registered Door Supervisors

Jamie O'Keefe has spent most of his adult life working within different areas of Security through the late 70s, 80s, and 90s. A majority of this time has been spent working the doors of Pub's, Clubs, and Live music venues within the heart of London's night-life. Although his role is now mainly within the education and training of security awareness within the leisure and retail industry. He has also spent much of his time working within some of the seediest back street clubs within London's notorious East End and Soho, dealing with people from all walks of life. Jamie is also a 7th Dan Black belt and Self protection instructor and spent his last few years relaxing from his nights on the door, by writing his first book 'Dog's don't Know Kung fu - a guide to female Self Protection.' This focused on his many years as a Self Protection instructor plus his 28 year study and analysis of the martial arts. He then went on to research and write this book 'Old School-New School' which focuses on the changes and evolution of the Bouncers of old, to the modern day Door Supervisors. This book covers the areas of Criminal and Licensing law, drugs, first aid, self protection, fire safety, the councils training requirements, along with many of Jamie's own personal reflections and thoughts on Bouncers and the role of Door supervisor's. If security within the leisure industry affects you or the safety of the environment within which you work - no matter how remote, you should read this book. It's a Blueprint for the future of Security!

Available from New Breed Publishing – mail order www.newbreedbooks.co.uk

New Breed, Po box 2676, Romford, Essex, RM7 0WA

Wild Thing: The True Story of
Britain's Rightful Guv'nor (Paperback)

Lew Yates

Due out

8 Jan 2009

The East End Villain they couldn't kill!

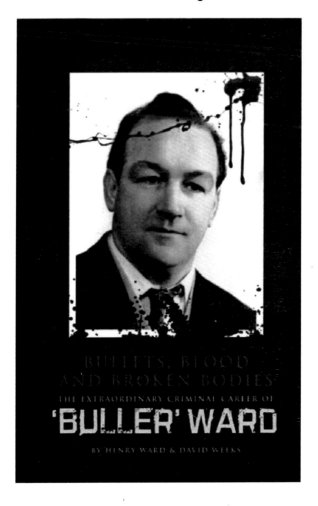

**Henry ' BULLER' Ward
Out Now!**

Want to write a book?

If you have a story to tell, a training program to record in print, or anything you want preserved in print for any reason; Please contact us to see if we can help you out.

You don't have to be a known name.

Millions of people could see your book on Amazon and will be able to order it through any bookshop

*Contact **Jamie O'Keefe***

jamieokeefe@tiscali.co.uk

New Breed Publishing – mail order

www.newbreedbooks.co.uk

New Breed, Po box 2676, Romford, Essex, RM7 0WA